TEACUPS

in the

ASHES

CARRYING A DREAM WHEN
LIFE FALLS APART

Written by Amy Smathers

First Edition 2025

Book Cover Design and Interior Formatting by 100Covers.

ISBN: 978-8-218-78888-9 (paperback)

*To the reader who is carrying a dream and wonders
if it will ever actually come to pass...
Jesus will be found faithful.*

Table of Contents

Preface

Dear Reader:

This book is for the person who is carrying a dream in their heart from the Lord, but they feel so overwhelmed that they don't know where to start.

I wrote this book at a time when I was building something too, because it was the book my younger self needed on the journey. Maybe it was meant to be—I grew up in Los Angeles, a city marked by Hollywood's bright lights and dreamers who often discover that the path to realizing their dream is filled with seemingly impossible obstacles before it finally comes to pass.

What I didn't realize when I set out to launch my own lifelong dream of starting a nonprofit, and even writing this very book, is that every time we have a big, impossible dream to change the world, often unexpected challenges appear and throw a wrench in our plans. At times the journey has been exhilarating and at other times it has felt so overwhelming, like I was following God into a dark unknown.

In the process of carrying my dream I faced so many delays, disappointment, self-doubt, and countless days that felt like giving up. I wonder if you might have faced these times too? Then, right as I launched my nonprofit, I faced the hardest season of my life when tragedy hit our family as fires destroyed our home, all our belongings, and the community I had called home my entire life.

We all have dreams, but then *life* has a way of getting in the way sometimes, doesn't it? The reality is that when we start, there is so much anticipation within us, but as challenges appear our hope fades and we can become weary.

In these pages we are going to talk about what to do when our faith wanes on the hard days. Together, we'll explore the question: **How do we carry the dreams God has given us to completion, cross the finish line, and pursue the very thing He's called us to with bold faith when life looks different than we imagined?**

Throughout these pages I don't come to you as an expert or someone who has "arrived" at the pinnacle of their career, but as someone walking alongside you as you write your own story. We'll start on our journey together by talking about comparison and inadequacy. Do you struggle with looking around you, and it seems like everyone else is thriving but you're still figuring it out? Or maybe you're like me and you almost disqualify yourself *before you even start?*

As leaders it's so easy for us to feel like we don't measure up or we'll never be "enough." But friend, you absolutely are. We'll unpack what Jesus says about our inadequacies and our "not enoughness," from imposter syndrome to social media, and we'll explore how it's really a superpower that can drive our leadership. We'll also discuss how the great leaders of the Bible, like Moses and Abraham, asked so many of the same questions about their own identity as leaders.

Once we determine how and why we're called, we're going to talk about what it looks like to move forward with faith and persevere through the storm. When challenges come, how can we have enough endurance to run our race? Along the way, we'll talk about what it looks like to heal and how our own unique story—even our deepest pain—can become what propels us forward into the future God has for us.

Next, we'll talk about spiritual practices that make us stronger and healthier leaders. What spiritual practices or rhythms can help us to keep moving forward so we don't get stuck, and we can keep the faith?

Finally, we'll talk about legacy. Once we know what we're called to, who we are called to, and why, we're going to talk about what it looks like to build an eternal legacy for the kingdom of God. As we look back on what we are building and dreaming about—be that a business, a family, or starting our own organization—we'll look at how we can do that faithfully in a way that honors God.

My hope is that whether you're just starting out or as things come up along your own journey, you'll be able to return to these pages and find a safe space where your soul is encouraged.

Friend, I believe that if you are reading this book, it's for a reason and that there is a courage, a resolve, and a resilience deep within you that you may not even see yet. I have spent hours praying that the right people would pick up this book. I pray that you would also be inspired to know that there are millions of people just like you who are dreaming with purpose and for a better future for them and for their families as they take big, messy steps of courage alongside you.

Those God-sized dreams and purpose inside of you? They're there for a *reason*. Throughout these pages I want to be part of your inner circle to encourage you, inspire you, and remind you that you were meant to fly.

God saw all of your weaknesses, setbacks, and your lowest moments, and he still picked you to do something for such a time as this. It's going to be a journey, but let's get through the mountains and valleys together. Sometimes, we just need someone else who has gone before us to believe in us and remind us that we're able to cross the finish line.

If you were here, I'd make you tea with honey or some of my famous chocolate chip cookies that my husband loves so much. They're big, flat cookies that fit in the whole palm of your hand with melted chunks of chocolate and a pinch of sea salt on top (the *best* way to have cookies in my opinion!). I'd set up a little table for us as the sun sets with bistro lights above and birds chirping in the distance. We'd laugh and talk about the real and hard and true things, and I'd wipe your tears away as we talk about the journey and what it has really been, the good and bad things you've been afraid to share with anyone else but yourself.

So, let's run our race together. I want to be that person for you as you read these pages. Let's run *hard*. And let's build a kingdom legacy that lasts for generations. You can do it, friend. On the other side of your obedience there are so many people looking for the hope that you alone carry. I'm so excited for this journey you are on, and I'm so honored to be a part of it with you.

With all the love in the world,
Amy

Throughout this book, you will learn about the community pictured above that I was so fortunate to call home growing up. This picture (also on the cover of the book) shows the area where I grew up right before it all burned. This view is so close to my heart and it still takes my breath away.

On January 7, 2025, the historic Palisades fire broke out in LA. Less than 45 minutes after the fires started, this was the view from my parents' home before they evacuated. Little did we know that our lives were about to change forever...

The next day, this is what was left of our home. This photo is taken from the vantage of our living room, right where our Christmas tree once stood. We had been sick over the holiday, so everyone's gifts were still wrapped under the tree. Without any buildings in the neighborhood, the remaining trees and mountains now remind me of home.

PART I

TRUSTING THE GOD WHO CALLS US

CHAPTER 1

Introduction

Have you ever looked back at your life and seen the ruins of something that you thought would always be there? Perhaps it's a breakup, the loss of a loved one, a divorce, even the loss of a dream? How are we supposed to carry on—never mind lead—when unimaginable suffering and loss happens in our life? And how do we still follow God faithfully when it feels like the life we thought we'd be living has crumbled around us?

So many of us have that one dream burning in our hearts, that thing we just know we were *created* to do. We keep it on the back shelf of our minds for years, sometimes even decades. Maybe we share it with a spouse or a close friend. Then, right when we're ready to set out and do what we feel God is calling us to do, something happens that turns our world upside down. That's what happened to me.

Right as God told me to step up as a leader and embark on my lifelong dream of starting a global nonprofit, I encountered the hardest season of my life. Then, as I tried to work through it and was ready to launch, *life* hit us again and we faced unthinkable tragedy.

January 7, 2025 is a day I will never forget. That morning my mom called and said that there was a fire near their house in LA, just five miles north from where my husband and I lived.

Twenty minutes later, she called in a panic. The fire was spreading as winds over sixty miles per hour were fueling the flames right in the direction of their house. She was still recovering from a shoulder injury and was scrambling to pack things up to evacuate, asking what we should pack and what we should leave behind. It's a call that nobody wants to receive.

Flames continued to roll down the hill as thousands of people were now scrambling to leave the neighborhood, rushing into the streets with what they could of their belongings. The roads were so chaotic that people were literally jumping out of their vehicles, pets and babies in hand, and running for their lives. Bulldozers brazenly pushed cars into piles on the side of the road so that fire engines and emergency vehicles could drive through. It was sheer chaos.

Even though my husband Chad and I lived close by, with so much gridlock on the streets there was no way we could drive in their direction and help my parents evacuate in time. I called them back and said that even if they hadn't packed everything up, they would need to leave now so they could still get out of the neighborhood.

A piece of my heart broke.

As the day progressed, we started to live out our worst nightmare as we watched the fire blaze through the beloved community that I had called home my entire life. It seemed like every hour we lost something new. Houses were on fire for miles and miles, as far as the eye could see. And worse, nobody was there to extinguish the flames. On the news, authorities told us that the winds were so extreme that firefighters couldn't access most areas and that they had run out of water.

So instead, we sat and painfully watched our whole little world lit up in flames.

"Your elementary school is on fire!"

"The library is gone! The recreation park is filled with embers now."

"Our grocery store! Our church! The frozen yogurt shop! They're all on fire! We can't find anyone to help!"

Finally, around 6 p.m. that day, my sister called and said the words we hoped we would never have to hear: "It looks like the house is gone."

I wept. There are few words that can describe the kind of pain we felt that day. Hopelessness? Anger? Despair? Those words don't feel like enough. My parents had lived in our house for forty years—to that exact day—and it was the only house I had ever known. My husband Chad and I had just moved back to LA a few months prior to be closer to my parents, and we visited my parents' house every week. Almost all my belongings from the move were still in boxes there. Now, all of the memories from our childhood were gone in minutes and the fire was still growing, burning homes within half a mile of the apartment where Chad and I lived. I was in utter disbelief.

Maybe, there are no words to explain it.

As daylight came we could finally peer through the smoke to see what was left before we evacuated ourselves, and the damage was far worse than anything we could have ever imagined. Over 85% of our hometown of Pacific Palisades, California—a beautiful beach town wedged between the Pacific Ocean and the Santa Monica Mountains—had been completely flattened. The entire city infrastructure, from schools to churches and stores, was gone within about twenty-four hours.

Rows and rows of homes were burnt to ashes like something out of an apocalyptic movie.

Over the coming days and weeks, we received countless messages from family and close friends who had lost homes. Many of them were unable to return home to grab anything at all because the fire happened so quickly. People we loved had even passed away.

In all, I lost nearly everything I had ever owned, our parents were left with nothing but two small carry-on bags, and the neighborhood I had called home was almost completely flattened by the flames.

What hurt the most were the things that reminded us of the memories we had shared with others. Together we lost all our childhood photos and family videos, the markers of a life well lived.

We lost wedding rings and class rings, yearbooks, and family heirlooms, like the cross necklace with little pearls my mom passed down to me from her wedding day and my great aunt's cookbooks with all of her notes in the margin.

We lost letters and birthday cards from loved ones, my favorite sweater, my first Bible.

We lost the special china and champagne glasses we always said we would use for "special occasions." We even lost the little things that you don't realize will mean so much one day, like the little knick knacks you bring home from family vacations that become so much more precious when everyone is grown up and it's harder to get the family together again.

We lost our Christmas tree, topped with my favorite angel ornament that my sister and I adored. We lost all of our family Christmas gifts under the tree too.

Most importantly, we lost our place of comfort, safety, beauty, and community that made us feel so connected to the loved ones and neighbors around us. It was like losing the promise of a tomorrow that would never come.

In just one day, our lives were changed forever.

Examining the Ashes

We ended up evacuating for a few weeks with my parents. Our apartment down the road from my parent's house survived within half a mile of where the fire stopped, but the entire city of Los Angeles was shaken by the devastation that had happened not just in the Palisades fire, but in Altadena, Malibu, and beyond.

About a month after the fires, we decided it was time to go back to our property to go through the ashes where our house once stood for some closure. I couldn't get over the fact that we had just been at our family home two days before the fire to watch a football game together. Everything had seemed so normal. I can still remember waving goodbye to my parents as we drove down the street with the car windows down, breathing in the crisp ocean air as our goldendoodle Leo stuck out his head, floppy ears flying in the wind happily as we started down the Pacific Coast Highway. Now, everything that had once been there was unrecognizable.

Where would we start? I thought. Nobody can prepare you for a moment like this.

Unsure of what we'd find, I said a quick prayer. Quietly, I whispered, "God, please show up today. If you're really for us, will you speak to us in some way today? Will you show us something at the house?"

We suited up in our hazmat suits and masks. Each step felt heavy, like walking in a space suit across the moon. Deep breaths.

My stomach was in knots. I stood in quiet disbelief at the top of our old driveway and looked at the rubble. Where we had once sat around the kitchen table for family dinners and looked out onto the mountains, our windows had burst and now glass was sprinkled across the planter over trampled calla lilies.

Drywall had caved in over our garage and living room where my sister and I had always made up plays and dance performances for my parents. The only recognizable thing was our chimney and fireplace. We had just hung red velvet Christmas stockings there, but now the brick foundation of our chimney towered over charred nails and dirt as a stark reminder of what once was.

We started walking along the side of the property, passing the trees where my big sister and I had taken photos before school dances and the pavement where we rode our scooters as little girls.

As I looked to the left, the very first thing I saw was a statue of an angel in the dirt under a charred magnolia tree. Fully intact, this clay statue looked out onto the ruins like an angel guarding our home. I gasped. I'd never noticed it before, but now as it towered over the remains my eyes locked in on it. Jesus' presence was already here. In my spirit I felt Him say, "Even though the house is gone, my protection over your family never left."

The pressure in my chest lifted another inch, and we started walking through the rest of the ruins to find a few more items.

We continued to trek over nails, crisped drywall, and pieces of metal but it was almost impossible to decipher what anything was under the film of dusty grey ash. I asked God to show up again. Then, as we walked through my old childhood bedroom, I saw a flash of cobalt blue shimmering through the ash.

There – right on top of the rubble – was a delicately placed tea set and a pile of beautiful blue teacups. They were in nearly perfect condition, almost like someone had moved them there to have afternoon tea on top of the ashes.

These weren't just any teacups, they were some of my most prized possessions. I had gotten them in India when my dream to start a nonprofit was born twelve years prior. I had even bartered for them in a bizarre in New Delhi, and I remember vividly being so proud of the deal I had negotiated in broken Hindi. They were small, hand painted chai cups, and now the cobalt blue flowers along the rim sparkled as bright as ever in the winter sun. More than that, they were a reminder of the dream God had given me in India to commit my life to empowering vulnerable women around the world.

I felt God say, "Amy, do you see? You are always on mission. Because you were obedient to go to India and follow your dream, I kept these teacups for you." Next to them, there was also a small pile of painted porcelain doorknobs from the same bizarre. God said, "See! I kept them there too! The doorknobs are for the numerous open doors to come."

Our last find was funny. We found a single page from a cookbook that had belonged to my great aunt Mary. She was born on the Greek island Lesvos, and she recently passed away, but we inherited a huge stack of her Mediterranean cookbooks. I used to love leafing through them and seeing her notes in the margin where she had marked her favorite recipes. As I looked closer at the page, I could see it was a page from a Tuscan cookbook about how to cook lamb. If you know anything about Greeks, they love their meat! I laughed and imagined her up in heaven looking down on us. We had always loved her elaborate family dinners. God said, "Don't forget hospitality and family. *Home* happens around tables."

I still find it miraculous that those delicate teacups were laid out so carefully across the ash. All five of them were perfectly in order like they had never been touched. Everything else in the house was destroyed by flames that reached over one thousand degrees. And how was it possible, I wondered, that a single page of my cookbook survived after it had rained so much since the fires? Surely that had to be the Lord.

This was one of the single most important moments I would have after the tragedy changed our lives forever, and God used it to speak a message that I believe is not just for our family but for everyone.

You see, our hopes and dreams for the future are a lot like those teacups.

At first glance they are so beautiful. They have intricate details, and each one is unique and special in its own way. But they are also fragile and delicate.

These teacups sitting in the ashes are like our dreams when we go through the obstacles of life. How do we protect our dreams and see them across the finish line when it feels like everything in our lives is burning around us?

January 7, 2025 was a day I'll never forget. But before we sift through the ashes, let's talk about where it all began.

CHAPTER 2

My Story

I was born in a Christian home in Los Angeles where our family attended a Presbyterian church every week. We grew up around Sunday school and Vacation Bible School in the summers, so I had grown up around people of faith, but over time it felt more like a family tradition than a personal relationship with Jesus.

I attended an all-girls high school in LA and was so excited to start my freshman year at Tufts University in Boston, where I planned to major in International Relations. I relished the new experience of living on the East Coast, where my mom grew up, for the first time in my life. And as someone who has always loved school, I couldn't wait to meet other students who were also passionate about current events around the world. From a young age I had always dreamed that I would one day become Secretary of State so I could make positive change and help others.

However, my first semester didn't take off quite how I had expected. Within a few weeks I was faced with a difficult personal challenge and found myself with a handful of strangers I was just starting to get to know. I kept going to class and acting like everything was going well on the outside, but on the inside, I didn't know how to process what had happened. I knew I needed God but didn't know how to find him in this new context. Because I had grown up in church I decided to go to a meeting of Intervarsity, a campus ministry where my sister had come to faith a few years prior while a student at Stanford University. I figured I'd just slip out of the meeting before anyone noticed if I wasn't feeling the message. But, as always, God had very different plans.

The first mistake was I didn't realize there was an "icebreaker" activity where I'd have to introduce myself to someone. For our icebreaker that week we were supposed to play rock, paper, scissors with the person next to us, but instead of saying each one we'd say our name instead. Eventually, as over a hundred people all played the game together, there'd be a face-off between two people.

Much to my frustration, I was one of those two people. So much for blending in! Over a hundred college students crowded around me and another other girl, shouting our names and jumping up and down. Then, I won! Now the *entire* room not only knew I was the new girl, but now they also knew my name. Oops, it was too late for me to leave! So I decided to stay a little more, and the sermon that day took my breath away.

The speaker shared the story of a friend who had been sexually assaulted in college and discussed how Jesus meets us in our pain. He talked about the story of Lazarus and how Jesus meets us in our darkest moments. He described how Jesus wept in that story of the Bible, and that's how he believed Jesus would have responded to his friend, too. I remember feeling like God himself was talking to me and I knew it wasn't an accident. I reluctantly decided to take one small step and to sign up to attend my first campus Bible study that week.

Every Monday, we came together and studied the book of Matthew, which talks about the life and ways of Jesus. Almost every week we talked about different miracles in the Bible and how we could live more like Jesus did. The funny thing is, I was always hesitant to attend our Bible study, but the more I showed up the more I realized that the students there were very different from anyone else I'd met on campus.

How is it that they're not worried about anything? I remember thinking a couple months in.

The Christians in my Bible study didn't seem stressed or anxious like so many of the students around me, not even during finals! And they carried this joy, peace and an all-knowing sense that everything was okay. It was incredible and I wanted what they had.

Are You In or Are You Out?

At the end of the semester my Bible study group invited me to join them for a conference called Urbana. It was going to be hosted in St. Louis, Missouri that year, and they were bringing nearly 20,000 college students together from around the country to talk about biblical justice, missions, and how God was moving around the world. Quite honestly, I didn't have anything else to do for winter break and hanging out with friends sounded fun, so I signed up.

I made it to the conference, but when I walked in, that same hesitation hit again. The venue was so different from the quiet Presbyterian church I had grown up in, where most of the music was played on an organ. The stereos were blasting worship music so loud I could hardly hear myself talk or even think. Strobe lights blasted flashes of light through the stadium as everyone else seemed to be lifting up their hands in worship. And while I'd met a few Christians in college at this point, I'd definitely never seen so many young Christians my age who loved Jesus and wanted to follow him with their lives. In fact, growing up in LA I couldn't even think of a single practicing Christian I'd met in my middle school or high school combined.

It was all so new and different that I started thinking through an escape plan to run back to our hotel room and take the first flight back home. Exasperated and confused, I cried out to God as we finally got back to our hotel room. I pulled the covers over my head and silently prayed, "I don't want to be here! But, God, those students also have something that I don't. They worship with their hands in the air, and they seem so connected to you. Yet I've been going to church for so many years and I don't feel a thing. If I have to be here this week and I can't fly home, can you at least show me why I'm here?"

Pausing, something came over me and I asked a question I'd never asked before. "God, growing up I remember hearing that you died for me and rose again. But what does that mean, really? Can you show me why you had to die for *me* on the cross?"

It was a simple prayer and I fell asleep shortly after that. But little did I know, that quick question at the end of my prayer would be one of the most powerful and transformative things I would ever ask God.

Over the course of the next few days everyone in the conference went through the first few chapters of the book of John. I was still overwhelmed, but somehow, I resolved that if I had to be there, I might as well try to get something out of it. We heard speakers, including missionaries and pastors from around the world and went to breakout sessions to learn about justice issues like human trafficking and global poverty. My heart slowly started to open. I was so moved by the speakers' devotion to God, their trust in him, and the joy and peace that they all shared. Some of them were even interested in going overseas as missionaries. It was a totally different world and I felt like I was on the outside looking in.

Finally, on the second to last night of the conference we got to the last chapter of our text for the week in the book of John. All week we had learned about how Jesus took on human form and lived incarnationally, entering into people's worlds right where they were with miracles, healing and truth.

Now, in chapter 4 we were introduced to the story of a woman from a town called Samaria who was an outcast in her community. For all of the sermons I'd heard growing up, I'd never heard about this woman in the Bible before, and I was on the edge of my seat.

I learned that the Samaritan woman had a messy past and she went to the well to draw water in the middle of the day, likely to avoid talking to anyone else. There she met Jesus. This woman was disillusioned, perhaps a little like me at that conference, and she was carrying a load that nobody but Jesus could see within her. So as Jesus met her there, he asked her for a simple drink of water and they started a conversation. Then, as he looked her in the eyes, Jesus spoke into her past and said that he can offer her "living water." He knew things about this woman that no other stranger should know, including that she'd been married five times and now was living now with a different guy. There's a lot of shame in her story, especially in this culture, but rather than calling her out on it, Jesus met her with love and compassion.

The most powerful part of the story? This woman who everyone else cast aside is the first person in the *entire* Bible who Jesus tells that he is the Messiah.

Exasperated and overjoyed, the Samaritan woman runs back to her community and shares this good news with anyone who will listen. What's wild to me about this story is that she came for a simple need—water—and her whole world changed. Because Jesus had now entrusted her with this information, her entire life and position in society changed too.

Through this interaction with Jesus, this woman threw off her shame and brokenness and she found freedom. Even more so, she became one of the most important people in *history* because she delivered this news of a Messiah that they waited generations to receive.

What jumped out at me that night was that she was carrying shame from her past. I hadn't told anyone, but the reason I had first attended campus ministry was because I had been sexually assaulted during one of the first weeks of college. For months I had been holding the secret in and carrying so much shame. Yet as I heard the messages, I also felt a conviction growing in my own heart that I needed a Savior too, just like her.

Jesus walked across the desert in the heat of day to comfort this woman and show her compassion, I thought. And he did the same for me when he died for me on the cross. He didn't see her story out of judgement, he saw the woman of God and the leader he had created her to be.

As the sermon came to an end, my mind was spinning. Something shifted in my heart and I felt a nagging tug to have someone pray for me. I'd never done anything like that before, and I'd also never been in an environment like this before where other young people prayed, too. I walked into a small prayer room and took a seat. I was paired off with a girl who was around my age to receive prayer. She asked how she could pray for me and out of nowhere I felt a voice, almost like an inner knowing or intuition, say, "Tell her what happened to you this past semester."

The words suddenly poured out of me as I shared nervously what had happened to me at school earlier that year. Here was something I had kept down for so long and thought I had moved past, but hot tears rolled down my cheek as I described everything that I had experienced. Then, as she prayed over me, something happened. I felt a warmth overcome my body and bring comfort. It's hard to describe in words but I felt like this load, a heavy depression, was lifted off of me. I heard that soft voice again that I somehow knew was Jesus telling me that he was giving me a clean slate and making me new. "Amy, I love you. You are made clean and white as snow," I heard. "You get a whole new start in life."

This voice wasn't audible—it was almost like a *knowing*—and it was so kind. It was so far from the words I would normally use every day, and it was a feeling of deep healing unlike anything I'd ever experienced before. I knew it was Jesus and I wanted to have a fresh start with him more than anything else in the world. I knew I had been sinned against, but I had also sinned in my own life, and I needed a Savior. I confessed my sin and prayed to receive him as Lord of my life. The whole exchange was so quick, but as I walked out I knew deep down that my life was never going to be the same. As the next session started a few minutes later, I ran back into the auditorium. I fell to my knees and lifted my hands in worship. I was made *new* in Christ. Here I had been days ago feeling so out of place and now I was a believer too. I finally understood!

I get it now, I thought, as I looked around the stadium. *I know why everyone has their hands up. I know why they believe in Jesus. I understand why he had to die on the cross for me, and I just want to worship him and thank him with my whole heart.*

Receiving the Invitation

This is the Jesus I met for the first time that day I decided to give my life to him. What I learned that day is that we can whole-heartedly trust him. He is a God who comes *to* us just as the Bible teaches us in John 1: "The word became flesh and dwelt among us" (John 1:14). He knew what I needed and encountered me in such a powerful way that changed me from the inside out.

Most importantly, he is a God who doesn't sit idly by as we are hurt, abused, or in pain. Unlike any other world religion, this is a God who chases after us and consoles us in our deepest pain. He loves us back to life until we know that we are not defined by our past, but we are precious and we belong to him.

When he comes to us, he comes with mercy, not judgement. I think so many of us are afraid to come to Jesus because we are afraid to be judged, but this exchange was such a beautiful picture of peace, mercy, and healing. The Bible says exactly what I have found to be true: "For God so loved the world that he gave his only Son, so that everyone who believes in him may not perish but may have eternal life. For God did not send his Son into the world to condemn the world, but in order that the world might be saved through him" (John 3:16-17). Where I had felt afraid and unworthy, the Lord had so much compassion and drew me back to him.

If you are reading this and you are carrying something heavy or want to know Jesus more, I believe he came for you too, not out of judgment but in mercy and to bring new life. You too can have a taste of this living water and experience his all-consuming and healing presence. If this story has struck a cord in your heart, join me in praying this simple prayer.

Dear Lord Jesus, I believe in You. I know that I am a sinner, and I believe that Jesus Christ died for my sins and rose again. I repent for my sins and for trying to live my life without you as my foundation. I ask for your forgiveness and I receive You, Jesus, as my Savior and my Lord. I invite You to come into my heart and life. Thank you for saving me. Will you now make me a new creation in Christ. Amen.

If you are reading this and you are walking with Christ but want to go deeper in your faith, here is a prayer for you.

Dear Lord Jesus, I want to know you more deeply. I need your healing presence and grace in my life. I give you my pain. I know you see and understand it all. Will you show me more of your peace and more of who you are? Will you remind me why you died on the Christ for me and just how you see me? Amen.

We Make Plans, God Laughs

Towards the end of my senior year of college, I started to pray about where I would work after graduation. God had done so much on our campus in my time there as a new Christian, from launching our first ministry in the Greek and athletes' communities to seeing full-on revival in our prayer meetings. Now, after interning at the State Department in Washington, D.C. between my junior and senior years of college, I was ready to follow God wherever he led me next. I was sure that I wanted to work in foreign policy in DC next as I pursued the dream I'd had as a little girl to become Secretary of State one day.

Yet, God had a different set of plans. I once heard the phrase, "When we make plans, God laughs," and that couldn't have been truer for what he was doing in my life. He was about to throw a giant curveball that would change the trajectory of my life forever.

The change started out small. When I returned to Boston after living in DC, I had this strange experience happen to me every time I prayed. I would envision a map of India every time I prayed about my next steps. It happened when I prayed at night, at church on Sundays, and every time in between, but it was just so random. Then it became increasingly specific, a map of the country with a red pin placed over a city in the west.

Is it Delhi? Mumbai? I wondered.

I didn't know a ton about India, but I at least knew a few major cities, and this picture did not pinpoint any of them. This same picture, a light-yellow map of India with a red pin, kept popping up in my mind all the time for two months, but I didn't tell anyone because I was so sure that I was moving to DC at the end of my senior year.

Finally, that fall, I went to a gathering for college students, and we all went out for pizza. One of our pastors, Jon, happened to be sitting across the table from my friends and me, and he asked if I had decided on any plans after graduation, and if I would consider global missions.

In the back of my head, I thought, "*No way! I'm moving back to DC!*"

But then he said something that caught my attention.

"My sister, Amy," he said, "has the same name as you! How funny is that! She's a missionary in India, can you believe that? She works with women, including some who are victims of human trafficking. You guys have a similar heart for anti-trafficking work, maybe I can connect you guys sometime."

His words stopped me in my tracks. I thought back to the map of India. And she had my name? It was just a little too on the nose.

"Where exactly in India does she live?" I asked, with a tinge of hesitation in my voice.

"Indore!" he said.

"Where's that?" I'd never heard of it before, so I asked him to show me a map.

Jon pulled up a map on his phone and typed in the name of the city where his sister lived. As he showed me the location, I gasped out loud.

On his phone was the map I had been seeing when I prayed for the past two months, down to the light-yellow background and a red pin. *Right* where I had seen it every time I had prayed. It was a perfect match.

Mapping Out the Future

I wish I could say I obeyed God, changed all my plans, and signed up to go to India right then and there. But I didn't. I was stubborn, and I made God chase me down as I continued pursuing my job in DC.

That November, one month after my conversation with our pastor, I got invited back to DC for the opportunity of a lifetime.

"*This is my time!*" I thought. "*It's all coming together!*"

When I was an intern, a leader at the State Department recruited me to support a new initiative for the Kimberley Process. This international certification system was established in 2003 to prevent the trade of conflict diamonds, or "blood diamonds." They are used to finance terrorists and rebel movements against legitimate governments.

By some amazing miracle, a colleague came across a project I created for school that was posted on YouTube. He was so impressed by it that he asked if I'd like to join one of the graduate interns spearheading research to shape the U.S. policy. We had an incredible time calling experts around the world, from executives at Tiffany's on Fifth Avenue in New York City to mining experts who worked in the rainforests in the Central African Republic.

The initiative we had researched and supported was now being implemented in 86 countries around the world. I was flying back to DC to volunteer and observe as it was voted through at the State Department's big plenary session, which brought all of the delegates together from around the world as they adopted this new protocol.

The event was a hit. I was so excited and convinced that this was a confirmation that God was going to provide a job here in DC! After the event, I walked through the State Department entrance and across Constitution Avenue to the Lincoln Memorial. I'll never forget sitting on the Lincoln steps and watching the afternoon sun glimmer on the pond in the National Mall. The Washington Monument towered ahead as droves of tourists with cameras gawked at the sights around me.

Here I was back in DC. I made it back! Now, all my dreams were coming true. It was a moment. I started to pray and thank God.

Then, I asked, "Where will I work? God, can you make it happen?"

"What neighborhood should I move to? Will it be here in Foggy Bottom? What about DuPont Circle or Georgetown?"

These were all the neighborhoods near where I had interned, and each of them had its own special charm.

I didn't sense that God was saying anything in response to my questions. Five minutes passed, ten minutes, but he was silent. Eventually, I started getting hungry, so I decided to move on to the next line of business that would change the world: getting something to eat!

But something strange happened again. As I went to pick up my phone and punch in the address for Founding Farmers, my favorite restaurant where I had planned to meet a friend for dinner, I was stopped in my tracks. Even though I had typed in the restaurant's address, my phone somehow malfunctioned and pulled up that same map of India without me touching a single button.

"Surely it's a glitch," I thought.

But no matter what button I pressed, I couldn't pull up the map to get directions for my walk to dinner. The only directions my phone showed were the distance from DC to this pinned city in India.

I felt a conviction in my spirit. God was up to something, and it was a lot bigger than I had realized.

CHAPTER 3

No Turning Back

Over the next several months, I continued to see signs almost daily that pointed me back to India. Friends who knew nothing about my plans would recommend books about India. Suddenly, a visiting professor taught one of my elective classes at school. He was from—you guessed it—India. My church announced that a group would travel there, and I applied to join them. These small signs persisted every single day for an entire year. God was on the move.

Most importantly, through months of prayer, conversation, and reflection, God showed me loud and clear that my reason for going to India was connected to my own testimony. I had healed after my sexual abuse in college and seen him move in so many powerful ways. Now, he wanted me to learn about the state of human trafficking on the ground and to gain insight into how to help trafficking survivors there. I also sensed that I would one day start a nonprofit to help women around the world, including survivors. I didn't know exactly what it would do, but I knew deep down that he wanted to show them the way to freedom, just like he had shown me and the Samaritan woman.

Within a few months, I graduated college and traveled to northern India with a small group from the United States. I planned to spend the first ten weeks with the group, and when our program together ended, I hoped to stay longer on my own with an internship.

India is such a uniquely beautiful place, and we quickly made many new relationships with the people there as we helped teach English to middle school students. With help from locals, we learned enough Hindi to get around the city in rickshaws, wear kurtas (long, collarless tunics), and navigate the streets during the intense rainstorms that came with summer monsoon season.

As our ten weeks was running out, I strongly felt that God was calling me to move to Mumbai next before I returned to the U.S. Mumbai is one of the biggest hubs for human trafficking in the entire world, so I figured surely the best way to learn about relief would be to talk to organizations on the ground that were doing the work of rehabilitating survivors and see if I could work with one of them.

But there was a problem: I still didn't have a place to work or live in Mumbai by our ninth week. Still, I felt God would provide. Days before the end of the trip, he did—a beautiful apartment with a group of girls around the same age who were all doing different work to serve the city, from working with orphans to the older women in the community.

I moved in with them temporarily and relished what author Suketo Mehta calls the "Maximum City." Mumbai, or Bombay, is the home of Bollywood and the economic powerhouse of India, housing the Bombay Stock Exchange. As we trekked across the city daily, it almost felt like every sense buzzed to life around us in the loudest way— colors were brighter, spices were more potent, and cars were far more numerous. The city is one of the most unique places I have ever been, from the famous Gateway of India along the Arabian Sea to towering skyrises. It also has some of the most significant income inequality, with one of the highest numbers of billionaires in a city, as well as one of the biggest slums in the world, Dharavi.

My favorite part of living in Mumbai was the opportunity to connect with incredible organizations working to support trafficking survivors. It was one thing to read about human trafficking or learn about it in school, but a whole other thing to meet with the very leaders who were reshaping the lives of survivors. These incredible organizations offered counseling, trauma care, education, and more. Others worked with law enforcement officials to rescue the girls from these unthinkable horrors.

To give you a picture: Often these women are rescued in "raids" that take months of planning and are conducted by nonprofits in collaboration with local law enforcement and intelligence agencies. When they are set free, interviews reveal that many survivors have been kidnapped, falsely coerced, or sold into slavery by people they trusted, sometimes even their own family members, teachers, or sports coaches. Trafficked women end up in new cities—sometimes even in another country—where they often live in dark and unsanitary conditions, unable to receive access to education. They have little access to food or the outside world, and, in some cases, are even kept in cages or live in chains. It is heartbreaking in every way.

A few weeks later, God dropped another clue about why he had me leap to move there. As I started to ask questions about the work to support survivors, I learned that many rescued women returned to the red-light districts because they had nowhere else to go.

I was shocked. I thought back to the word the Lord had given me about showing other women who had encountered sexual abuse the way back to freedom.

You mean with all the effort that went into rescuing someone from trafficking, they would return to it? Wouldn't they want to stay free? How is this possible?

However, the decision of these women to return to this work wasn't an issue of what the women wanted; rather, it was a question of the resources that were available to them. With no education, no form of physical education, no financial stability, and often living in a new city where they know nobody, these women have no other choice but to go back into prostitution and sex trafficking.

My heart broke as I considered the freedom I wished they could experience compared to the conditions they faced every day.

How is it that we could live in freedom, while these women live enslaved in plain daylight and even in the middle of one of the world's largest cities? Imagine if this were your daughter, sister, or friend. I knew deep down that God's heart for these women was for them to be leaders and have a voice, for them to know that they are precious and loved, created in the image of God, and yet, here they were living through unthinkable trauma.

What would their lives look like if they were different? Who could they become if they hadn't been trafficked here? I wondered.

As I did more research into human trafficking, I learned that while more organizations have begun to raise awareness in the last decade and even conduct rescue operations, organizations that focus on rehabilitating rescued women for the longer term are still scarce. Many of these women needed serious counseling services, trauma care support, transitional housing and shelter, and job training services. These processes can take years and require millions of dollars in funding.

At that time, it was reported that almost 50 million people were living in modern-day slavery, making it one of the most significant problems that our generation was going to face in this century.

Here I was, a twenty-one-year-old girl with a heart to see change but little to no work experience. I wasn't a social worker, a psychologist, or a doctor who could provide direct services. Who was I to be a leader who could provide a solution? Yet I continued to think of these women daily. It was something I couldn't shake.

Something had to be done, somehow. I decided then and there that I would find a way. I would get the training. One day I would provide a pathway to freedom for these women through a global nonprofit. I knew I couldn't fix this enormous problem alone, but if I could impact even a few girls by starting a new organization to support them, it would be more than worth it. So, I started asking a lot of questions everywhere I went.

I asked questions like, *"If one woman gets a job, how will her children or her family be impacted? And if her daughter could go to school, what outcomes would change for her?"*

That grew to bigger questions, like *"What are the most effective ways to reduce global poverty? What does that data say about the impact of empowering women and young girls across an entire community? What interventions have worked, and if they haven't, why not? Are there better solutions to address some of these challenges?"*

I discovered that the problem was far worse and more widespread than I knew. To give you a sense, one in every 10 women is currently living in extreme poverty. By 2030, projections show that 8 percent of the world's female population, or 342.4 million girls, will still be living on less than $2.15 a day. Women are also more likely to be food insecure, have limited access to education, and experience violence, with experts estimating that 245 million women and girls experience physical and/or sexual violence by their partner.

However, the good news is that the data also suggests—overwhelmingly—that investing in young girls and women has a lasting impact well beyond each intervention.

Amid this research process, I quickly realized that in affecting the life of just one female survivor, we could change not only the trajectory of her life for the better. It had the potential to transcend to her entire family, community, and impact generational legacies for years and years to come.

This realization was empowering but also sobering. My big dream was to create a global nonprofit organization that I would call The Well Initiative. It wanted to connect it back to my testimony of healing, so I decided it should be named after the same story of the Samaritan woman at the well in John 4 that I had heard the night I became a Christian. In my heart, I knew God had allowed me to experience freedom. I wanted to bring that same sense of healing and freedom to thousands of other women worldwide who needed it the most.

I hoped that the women who went through our program could be spiritually free and have safe work that enabled them to be free economically. I also envisioned what impact this would have. Like the Samaritan woman, their identity would no longer be defined by the deep shame and pain from their past, but rather the realization that they, too, were made to be leaders, world changers, and strong women of God with purpose and a new hope for the future.

My experience in India highlighted—as the rest of my career would later confirm—that there was consensus around what the world's biggest problems were, and funding was even on the table, but we lacked the collaboration and networks needed to address them effectively in our generation.

It was also time to make a change and start a greater movement for a more holistic, empowered approach addressing these challenges. And instead of relying on governments that used an aid-based model, I also sensed God showing me that this model would blend entrepreneurship, faith, ministry, and justice work. We needed an approach that would bring together nonprofits and other actors, like businesses and social entrepreneurs, and could be executed more sustainably. Then we could bring everyone to the table together and find pathways to collaborate in specific sectors, like economic empowerment, to make change together. As big as these goals were, I believed that the answers to these massive questions were within reach.

Often, when God shows us a problem, it's because we're meant to be part of the solution.

And God was about to do it, just not in the way I expected.

CHAPTER 4

The Big Questions
We All Ask:
Who Am I to Lead?

Have you ever been so excited about something you felt God was calling you to do, only to feel completely crazy the next moment? Me too.

Even when God calls us to something, there are still many moments where we will wrestle with God. Or, often, it looks much different than we ever anticipated.

After two months of living in India, I returned to the U.S. While I had hoped to stay for up to a year there, my plans took a turn when I got sick and I had to come home after just a few short months. Suddenly, I started having stomach aches that were so severe I could hardly walk or eat.

I had no choice but to go back home and recalibrate. Now, dealing with a new sickness that even doctors in the U.S. couldn't diagnose, I was questioning everything. I was so angry at God that I had followed him faithfully, and yet living in India didn't work out like I thought it would. I had listened to God's voice, and taken a step of great obedience and courage, only to end up right back at home in the States, asking God what was next. It wouldn't be until years later that I would finally learn that what I had experienced in India was a flare-up of a rare autoimmune disorder with no cure called Crohn's disease.

Even though everything had turned out so differently than I had anticipated and I wasn't able to stay in India to work, the women I had learned about there stayed at the forefront of my mind. I was determined to treat every next step in my career as an opportunity to get one step closer to my goal of providing them with alternative livelihoods so that they could finally live in freedom.

However, I was now jobless, had an autoimmune disease, and ultimately was left with more questions than I had answers. In addition to all of that, I was consistently facing that common shadow: imposter syndrome.

During that time in my life I asked questions like, *"Who am I to start an organization of that magnitude? Why is this illness coming up now? And if I take the leap to go after this dream, how am I going to do it? But most importantly, God, what the heck is going on?"*

You want me to lead, God? You've given me this dream? Who am I?

I've met leaders in saris and suits, male and female, young and old, yet at the end of the day, I've found that most of us have the same inner dialogue. Whether or not we say it aloud, we all secretly wonder, *can I do this? Would (insert name here) do a better job than me? Do I measure up enough to be here? Do I have the right talents, speaking abilities, personality, (fill in the blank)? Am I enough?*

The good news is we aren't alone in it. In fact, as I went through this journey of self-doubt and faced newfound obstacles to the dream I was carrying, I realized that two of the most important leaders in the Bible—Moses and Abraham—were a lot like most of us when we were first called. They were hesitant, afraid, and unsure at times—so human.

So, friends, this is where we are going to start on our journey together. Moses and Abraham were both called to do huge things for the Kingdom of God that changed the course of history, and yet they both struggled to reconcile their faith in God with their fear and doubt that God would use them to fulfill their given assignments. They faced many obstacles, whether external or internal. Sound familiar?

As we look at their stories, we will focus on two universal leadership questions that I believe we all ask as leaders:

1.) Who am I to do this?

2.) How do I know that you will show up, God?

Learning from Moses' Story

In the book of Exodus, God calls Moses into one of the biggest assignments in the Bible. So often when we think about Moses, we think about the parting of the Red Sea and the man who led the Israelites out of slavery—but do you ever think of him as a shy, unsure, or reluctant leader?

In the Bible, God says to Moses:

> I have indeed seen the misery of my people in Egypt. I have heard them crying out because of their slave drivers, and I am concerned about their suffering. So I have come down to rescue them from the hand of the Egyptians and to bring them up out of that land into a good and spacious land, a land flowing with milk and honey... So now, go. I am sending you to Pharaoh to bring my people the Israelites out of Egypt. (Exodus 3:7-10)

Pause. You'd think Moses would be jumping up and down with excitement, right? Here God is telling him that he's heard the cries of the Israelites and he's announcing his rescue mission to save them from years of living in brutal slavery. You would think he'd be running in circles and thanking God! But Moses doesn't do that. In fact, he doesn't miss a beat before he catches that last part—now *he* (Moses) is supposed to go before Pharaoh, the most powerful man in the land. Right away, Moses feels immense intimidation and fear.

"*Who am I* that I should go to Pharaoh and bring the Israelites out of Egypt?'" Moses asks (Exodus 3:11).

If you've been in church for a while you've probably heard this story many times over. Flash forward a bit and the story goes that the Israelites were enslaved in Egypt, and they went through a long journey that eventually led them to a Promised Land, Israel, a wild journey that takes up much of the Old Testament we read today.

But by the next chapter, Moses has upped his game before God. He's now moved on from asking "Who am I?" to resigning himself from this crazy role altogether. He wants a way out. In other words, he decided this whole thing is not going to happen at all. The Bible says:

"But Moses again pleaded, 'Lord, please! Send *anyone* else'" (Exodus 4:13, NLT, emphasis added).

Moses then said to the Lord, "Pardon your servant, Lord. I have never been eloquent, neither in the past nor since you have spoken to your servant. I am slow of speech and tongue" (Exodus 4:10).

The CliffsNotes version would explain here that Moses listed off his inadequacies (as if God didn't already know they existed). Moses was clearly feeling overwhelmed! Theologians believe that Moses may have had a speech difficulty. Either way, you can see lack of faith in his response. He simply can't see himself as the kind of leader that God saw him as, and he didn't even know that half of it and what was going to be involved!

God replied to Moses with a mic drop. God said, "Who gave human beings their mouths? Who makes them deaf or mute? Who gives them sight or makes them blind? Is it not I, the Lord? Now go; I will help you speak and will teach you what to say" (Exodus 4:11-12).

God reminds Moses that he created him. He created Moses' mouth, his ears, his eyes, and gave him all his abilities. He knew Moses in and out, and he was intimately familiar with all of Moses' weaknesses and inabilities.

What does Moses do next? Does he bow down before God, acknowledging his power as the Creator? Does he apologize and back pedal after telling God that he's essentially *wrong* and picked the wrong guy? Nope. In his own broken humanity, Moses says what I think most of us say initially when God calls us to do something really hard.

"Pardon your servant, Lord. Please send someone else," Moses says.

Wow. You've got to admit that Moses was gutsy to speak to God like that. This was God, who created all things in the universe! Yet what I secretly love about this exchange is that it's so *real*.

I don't know about you, but when God has told me in the past that I would be called to do hard things, like founding a nonprofit or even writing this book that you're holding, my first reaction was, "God, you've got the wrong girl. *Me?* You don't mean this girl on Instagram with an amazing New York Times bestsellers list? She's a great author! Or how about the one who is the best public speaker and tells the best jokes? I'd listen to her all day!"

And to that I just imagine that God so graciously stoops down, looks us directly in the eyes, and softly whispers,

"Yes, you. I created your most innermost being. I can count the hairs on your head and the tears that have fallen down your face. You. You have a story to tell. There are people who need you. *You, just the way you are."*

The Universal Question

Let's zoom out for a second. This story is about a man, Moses, who lived thousands of years ago. I think about the fact that he was a different gender, he wore different clothes (probably a long robe), and he existed in an entirely different culture and time in history. And yet, isn't his question the same one that we all ask of God? There's a huge lesson for us on our leadership journey in Moses' story.

"Who am I that I should go?" he asks.

Similarly, we ask questions like, *"Who am I* that you would put this dream in my heart and this call on my life?"

"Who am I that you would choose me to go on mission for you?"

"You want me to do this big thing? Broken, flawed, imperfect me? Surely I'm not the one you mean, God?"

If this scene played out in a movie, I imagine you'd see Moses looking behind himself to see if God was looking at his buddy standing a few feet back.

As I read this passage, I connect so much with Moses' questions. If he's anything like me I think he was really asking: *God has to mean that other guy and not me, right?*

These are the voices that play through our head. We think, *God, don't you know I'm not good enough for that?*

"*I'm not as holy as them. I'm not as smart as them. I'm not as strong as them. I'm not as charismatic, clever, or confident. I'm not a leader!*"

"Who am I to be a leader?" is the universal question we all ask.

TEACUPS IN THE ASHES

> *"Who am I to be a leader?" is the universal question we all ask.*

Like I talked about earlier in the chapter, that stinging feeling of self-doubt is probably the single biggest factor that kept me back as a leader when I first started out. If I'm totally honest, I still struggle with some of these thoughts sometimes and have to come back to the truth about what God has said about me and my calling.

Like Moses, we can ask questions like "Who am I" and still do it afraid if we're led by God's love.

In my own story it turns out that God had a really good answer to my first question: "Who am I to be a leader?" I wasn't ready for his assignment when he called me, but he slowly started chipping away at my fear so I could one day bring it into fruition.

But there was still another critical question: If I held up my side of the bargain, would God hold up his?

CHAPTER 5

The Big Questions
We All Ask:
How Can I Know?

Funny enough, after returning from India, I went straight back to Washington, D.C. I received my next big internship immediately after, and a few months later, I started my first job. Looking back, I imagine God laughing and saying, *"See Amy? My plans are good. I gave you a heart to be in DC, you just had to make a pit stop first!"*

For my first job, I worked in the U.S. Institute of Peace, across the street from the State Department. We even went over to their cafeteria for lunch sometimes! What's funny is that for over two years, my desk faced out onto big floor-to-ceiling windows overlooking the Lincoln Memorial—right where I had first prayed to God for a job in DC, and here I was living my answered prayer. Another God wink: I was working on the South Asia team, so it combined a mix of my time overseas in India and my previous experiences working in diplomacy in DC. Our team supported programs in Pakistan, Afghanistan, and *India*. You heard that right, India! God has a sense of humor.

We regularly hosted world leaders, civil society leaders, journalists, filmmakers, and activists at the Institute to learn what was happening on the ground. My favorite meetings, though, were always with the brave women who were working to bring peace in their communities, including many women serving in parliament in Afghanistan who had even survived assassination attempts from the Taliban and other threats. They were bold, courageous, and their passion for positive change was contagious. These experiences were transformational. Here I had been so mad at God for not allowing me to stay in India long-term, and now people from India and surrounding countries were flying to my new place of work, halfway across the world. Even though I wasn't overseas, God provided a front seat to learn more about global issues women were facing.

As time went on, I gained confidence that God's plans were still good and he was slowly molding me to become the leader he had called me to become in India. In other jobs I even had the opportunity to travel around the world and found myself sitting in foreign parliaments to meet with leaders there about stopping human trafficking and addressing major human rights issues—another full circle moment.

But I still had one big question: *"God, how do I know you will show up if I trust you?"*

Have you ever asked this too? You're in great company.

Abraham's Story

It turns out, Abraham—one of the most famous leaders in the Bible—asked this exact question when he was first called.

When we first meet Abraham in Scripture, he is already 75 years old. Genesis 11:28 tells us that Abraham's father, Terah, lived in Ur, an influential city in modern-day Iraq. Then Abraham's story really turns interesting at the start of Genesis 12.

In the first three verses, we see his call from God. The Bible says:

> The LORD had said to Abram, 'Leave your coun-
> try, your people and your father's household and
> go to the land I will show you. I will make you
> into a great nation and I will bless you; I will make
> your name great, and you will be a blessing. I will
> bless those who bless you, and whoever curses you
> I will curse; and all peoples on earth will be blessed
> through you. (Genesis 12:1 - 3)

But as we find Abram (later named Abraham) later in Genesis 15, he was a man who was called but had a lot of questions. God started their exchange by saying to Abram, "Fear not, Abram, I am your shield; your reward shall be very great" (Genesis 15:1).

I think God is doing a few things here. First, God said not to fear, but note that this was actually a command, not a question. Don't we all face fear when we're in a long waiting season? Aren't there so many "what ifs" that run through our mind? I think God saw that right away in Abram.

We are all infallible beings, and we are susceptible to fear, which is why God started here with Abram. What's interesting to me too is that God wasn't afraid of Abram's fear. He simply recognized that fear so he could get it out of the way and encourage Abram in this place of anxiety and worry.

Now I love the next thing God said! God said to Abram, "I am your shield." As in, you don't need to fear, Abram, *because* I am your shield. In other words, God declared that he can feel that fear, and God can feel it in Abram as he spoke to him, but that he was still his shield!

Last, God said, "Your reward shall be great." Now God had addressed Abram's fear, he's shown Abram that he's covered by the Lord, and then this huge promise dropped in Abram's lap.

Can you imagine hearing from the King of the Universe that you were getting a *great* reward? I wish I could be a fly on the wall to hear Abram's thoughts as this news was delivered. His reward shall be *great*.

Abram replied: "O Lord GOD, what will you give me, for I continue childless, and the heir of my house is Eliezer of Damascus?" . . . And Abram said, "Behold, you have given me no offspring, and a member of my household will be my heir" (Genesis 15:12).

And the Lord says: "This man shall not be your heir; your very own son shall be your heir. And he brought him outside and said, 'Look toward heaven, and number the stars, if you are able to number them.' Then he said to him, 'So shall your offspring be.' And he believed the LORD, and he counted it to him as righteousness" (Genesis 15: 2 -6).

Abram has a lot of questions in this passage. Don't we all? I'm right there with him. Yet God doesn't run from the questions just like he doesn't run away from Abram when he knows that he's fearful. As Abram cries out to God and asks how he will have a child, God takes him outside and tells him his descendants will be as numerous as the stars in the night sky.

This moment is one of the most famous moments in the Bible, and it's so beautiful. In this moment, I think God knows Abram is so in his emotions (fear, frustration, disappointment, confusion, etc.) that he knows he needs to do something that will captivate Abram's attention and awe. Descendants as numerous as the stars? That's billions! Can you even imagine? God wants to bring Abram direction—or maybe even re-redirection—and provision.

Isn't it interesting, too, that God doesn't really give Abram any concrete steps or directions, but instead he gives him a promise? Here I believe God wants to teach Abram about having faith, which Scripture defines as "confidence in what we hope for and assurance about what we do not see" (Hebrews 11:1, ESV). He's teaching Abram to see things on the *inside*—in his heart—before he sees it comes to pass on the *outside*, in his physical situation. This act of faith requires us to be present with God but it's also so much easier said than done.

Abram finally believes the Lord this time, and the Bible says that he (Abram) was counted as righteous. God sees his belief as deeply valuable.

As Abram is pondering this miraculous news about his descendants. God reminds him again who he is and what he's done. He says, "I am the LORD who brought you out from Ur of the Chaldeans to give you this land to possess" (Genesis 15:7). Again, God is saying, "I've got you! My son! I can do it!"

And now here's our question for this chapter. Abram asks, "Sovereign Lord, how can I know that I will gain possession of it?"

Isn't this the same question we all have? God gives us a promise or a word to hold onto, or maybe a friend speaks encouragement over us, and yet we all come back to this same question:

How can I know you're in it with me?

If you're like me, this is your question too.

As we step into this part of Abram's story, God has already shown up for Abram time and time again. He gave Abram a fresh vision for the future. He shared that he was going to do things only God could do because they were impossible to man. He's reminded Abram how powerful he is. And yet, he still has so many questions.

Me too. The real stuff in our walk with the Lord is questions like,

How can I know that God will really be faithful this time?

How can I know God heard our prayers?

How can I know God will do what he said he would do?

How can I know our situation will change?

How can I know God isn't going to just leave me in the dust?

Maybe you've walked with God for a long time—maybe a short time—but don't we all want to know *how?*

I've seen this to be so true in my life countless times where I've asked God for direction. As I write this, I think of my family trying to re-build after the fire burned our home. If I'm honest, I still have no idea how God will redeem it all as I examine the heaps of dirt that are piled where our family home once stood. I still get choked up when I drive through our old hometown and see the ashy ruins of the church I grew up in, the park I used to play in, or the Gelson's store where the bakery would offer us kids the most perfect sugar cookie with rainbow sprinkles as we shopped. There's been so much loss and our community is still grieving it in very real ways.

It's a bleak and very physical reminder of what was and that our story isn't done being written yet. I can only remind myself that whenever we see ruins in our life, it is the start of God building something new and for our good.

In moments like these, change feels impossible and waiting for God to move feels like walking in quicksand. Sometimes our situations look as impossible as Abram believing he and Sarai could conceive. Or sometimes it might be more conceivable, but we've been so beaten down by life and our own discouragement we struggle to believe again.

We need a move of God.

And that's where God is taking this whole exchange with Abram. God's response then, like it is now, was simply to trust him.

Abram's story works out in the end. In Genesis 17, God re-names Abram as Abraham, meaning "father of multitude." Abraham does have these descendants. And you know what's an even better spoiler? You are one of these descendants!

This passage encourages me so much because it reminds me that questions are part of the journey, even fear at times, and yet God has a track record of showing up with compassion, provision, and direction in the middle of our messiness. In fact, part of me wonders if this story was included in the Scripture for the very reason that God knew that centuries later, we—the descendants of Abraham—might face some of these very same questions that Abraham did.

The good news is that since our questions, like "How, God?" carry over, so can our faith. We too can have faith that pleases the Lord by trusting in him!

Now that we've talked about what it looks like to trust God, let's talk about how we can combat the inevitable inner dialogue that can keep us from moving forward. Aren't we also our own worst critics most of the time?

PART II

PERFECTLY IMPERFECT

CHAPTER 6

The Anti-Highlight Reel

You might be wondering what happened after I finally made it to Washington, D.C. and was finally living out what I thought I would be doing the rest of my life. Well, once again, God had different plans.

Seven years went by in DC. So, I'm not boring you with all the details, here's a version of my highlight reel during that whirlwind.

- My "yes" to Jesus brought me to a few other jobs that took me all over the world, from the State Department, the Pentagon, and the West Wing, to embassies and foreign parliaments. I was honored to meet child soldiers, ambassadors, generals, refugees, political prisoners, journalists, film directors, and humanitarian heroes working on the front lines to solve some of the world's biggest problems. It was amazing and it filled my passport!

- I got my master's degree at Georgetown University and completed a capstone project on economic empowerment programs for vulnerable women. Then we were faced with a global pandemic upon graduation while searching for a job. Yep, *that* pandemic. The one we're all still trying to forget.

- Thankfully, though, I met my husband, Chad, while I was back in LA for two weeks during the pandemic to visit family. It's a wild story: we had met four years prior in 2016 and were supposed to have our first date then. But shortly after we set our date, Chad felt like God told him he needed to be single for a while, and he had to *cancel our date!* So he did and we never saw each other. Four years later, we reconnected during the height of COVID, and the rest was history. I ended up moving from DC back to LA, and we dated for a little over a year before we married in the fall of 2021. Was it hard to leave DC? Definitely, but I'd take meeting my soul mate any day, pandemic and all.

- I still thought we could move back to the East Coast, but *plot twist!* We moved to the land of queso and barbeque: Dallas, Texas. As it turned out, God called us to move there right as we started our lives together as newlyweds. You'll hear a lot more about that Dallas season later, as it became a formative time for us and the dream that God had been speaking about since India.

Whew. Even sharing that on these pages is exhausting. Let's take a humor break.

The Canine Tornado

There I was—standing in front of a classroom of bright-eyed women, all ready to dive into a whole evening of leadership and ministry training—when a major disaster struck. Not a metaphorical disaster, A literal, furry, tail-wagging puppy disaster.

I had prayed for this moment, journaled, practiced my talk several times, and even color-coded my notes. I was finally chosen to lead our Women in Leadership Development program, affectionately called *WILD*, at our new church in Dallas. This was it—my moment—my big WILD debut.

The class started off perfectly. I'd spent hours preparing a message on the leadership of Moses (you know, parting the Red Sea, miracles, epic beards, a reluctant leader turned legend). I wore my favorite blue blouse and even snapped a pre-class Instagram post with the perfect vanilla latte, my outline, and a cute caption about how I was so grateful for what God was doing through these women. Under the dim lighting, the snack table looked beautiful. I was ready.

And then I saw the Ring notification. At first, I tried to ignore it. Maybe it was just the neighbors getting home? But then another one appeared. And another. Within a minute, eight notifications pinged. I glanced at my phone and saw the headline: "Motion Detected: Bedroom." My stomach dropped.

Our precious dog, Leo—our sweet, fluffy, crate-trained, and freshly groomed mini Goldendoodle—had gone wild. His traumatic haircut earlier that day had unlocked a new level of rebellion, and he was about to let us have it during this lesson. On the Ring cam, I watched in horror as he climbed out of his crate like a four-legged Houdini, sprinted across our white linen duvet, ran a victory lap around the carpet, peed, and then launched himself at the camera like he was auditioning for *Mission: Impossible—Puppy Protocol.*

Ten minutes later, on our break, I speed-walked to the bathroom and winced. I quickly tried using the speaker to tell him to quiet down and went through every command he knew, only to see Leo howling even more loudly at the camera.

I should have told the class. I truly wish I had. Inside, I was crawling and wanted to shout, "Hey ladies, minor emergency. My dog's staging a coup at home and may or may not be peeing all over our duvet, so see you next week!"

But I didn't share. I was still new. I wanted to impress the class, and I wanted them to take me seriously and see me as a responsible leader. Plus, my husband was next door teaching his class for men, blissfully unaware that we were minutes away from needing all-new IKEA bedroom furniture.

Just as I wrapped up my final section on "Leading with Courage in the Unknown," my phone buzzed again: one notification showing I received another like on my latte art Instagram post... and right beneath it, another motion alert of Leo climbing *back onto the bed*, barking at the camera.

It was poetic, really, and so ironic. On the outside, I was composed and confident, and on Instagram, I even had the perfect coffee shop filter. On the inside, I was full of chaos and self-doubt, completely frazzled.

Leadership lesson? Never let a curated image on social media convince you someone's got it all together. Behind every picture-perfect post is a lot of caffeine, a broken plan, and another woman just trying to figure it out along the way. We're all just doing our best.

Next time you're tempted to compare your life to someone's highlight reel, just remember someone might have written that shiny post while their dog was peeing on a pillow. Don't buy the lie of appearances. Don't give into the influencer illusion. Real leadership—and real life—is way messier. And honestly, I think it's far better.

A Comparison Generation

I think it's essential that we take a second to address the moment that we're in. More than any other time in history, our generation has been constantly bombarded by images of perfection that are photoshopped, filtered, and endlessly distorted to appeal to the masses online. In fact, studies show that the average American is exposed to 4,000 - 10,000 ads per *day*.[1] That's nearly double

---

1 Simpson, Jon. "Finding Brand Success in the Digital World." *Forbes*, 25 Aug. 2017, www.forbes.com/sites/forbesagencycouncil/2017/08/25/finding-brand-success-in-the-digital-world/. Accessed 7 Apr. 2025.

the number of ads the average person saw in 2007 and over five times as many ads as the average person saw in the 1970s![2] I know on my social media feed I'm constantly inundated with highlight reels of what seems to be perfection all the time, while my own life is far from it.

If I scroll through my feed today, I see post after post of picture-perfect families. They've got a big kitchen with a massive marble island, gold knobs on their cabinets, and that perfect farmhouse kitchen sink overlooking double paned French windows. Their fridge is organized in rainbow colors. They show photos from exotic family vacations where everyone looks happy and refreshed. Out of nowhere I think about the fact that we don't have children yet; my life feels so far behind and it feels like they're so far ahead, even though it's simply the season God has us in for now. No wonder we all set ourselves up against this unattainable standard.

We are now witnessing an unprecedented mental health crisis that is affecting young people, and it has everything to do with the way we compare and covet. This isn't a small issue. Every time we look at others and compare, we step away from our God-given destiny and identity. Here are a few statistics that might surprise you:

- One out of two girls as young as 6 to 8 years old want to be thinner.

- Cosmetic surgery on youth under the age of eighteen has tripled in a decade.

- Twice as many females compared to males are diagnosed with depression post-puberty.

---

2 King. "Hoot Design Company | a Women-Led, Creative Branding Agency." *Hoot Design Company | a Women-Led, Creative Branding Agency*, 2025, hootdesigncompany.com/brand-is-king. Accessed 7 Apr. 2025.

- About 65% of American women and girls have an eating disorder.[3]

- On average, males spend ten hours and fifty-eight minutes on social media, while females spend twelve hours and eleven minutes. [4]

We're all feeling the pressure to be perfect.

Influencing Others, Not Following Influence

This message has become even more potent for our social media generation where we've seen another layer of messaging about our worth and identity. Social media has given us so many complex narratives: Visibility equals success. Followers equals friends. Likes equals approval. With so much of us on social media, we constantly feel like we have to "curate" the perfect life online. Every vacation, life milestone, even time with others are captured in videos and posts for hundreds, thousands, and millions to see (depending on your following).

Meanwhile, as a woman I see culture tell us that we are to be CEOs and business leaders but also full-time moms who attend every soccer game. Think of your traditional housewife but then add titles like "girl boss," and you've got a perfect storm for unattainable standards. We're expected to have a (healthy, organic, farm-to-table) dinner on the table, homemade (but also gluten-free, dairy-free, keto-friendly) cookies after school, all while "keeping our figure" and our families in order. We're wearing makeup but it's

3 "Survey Finds Disordered Eating Behaviors among Three out of Four American Women (Fall, 2008)." *UNC Gillings School of Global Public Health*, 26 Sept. 2008, sph.unc.edu/cphm/carolina-public-health-magazine-accelerate-fall-2008/survey-finds-disordered-eating-behaviors-among-three-out-of-four-american-women-fall-2008/.
4 Foy, Carole. "How Much Time Do People Spend on Social Media in 2024?" *Twicsy*, July 2024, twicsy.com/blog/time-spent-on-social-media.

supposed to look like no makeup all while covering those wrinkles and marks that simply come from living life. Our outfits are supposed to be attractive but not too tight or short, not too masculine but not too feminine either. We're supposed to bear children but not carry pregnancy weight, and we're supposed to act confidently and boldly but not be seen as bossy, arrogant, or aggressive. To steal from a popular movie quote, we have to be "Everything, everywhere, all at once."

The labels we have agreed to are endless, and most of us run an exhausting mental marathon every day as we silently struggle with the expectations we feel we must meet. When will this end? How could we possibly feel enough—called and set free in the image of a loving and endlessly creative God—if we focus on this narrative that always has a laundry list ready for us on the ways we must improve to be fully accepted, known or loved? When will we finally call this out as not only unattainable, but *detrimental* to our mental and emotional health? That's why facing comparison head-on is so important to fulfilling the call and purposes God has uniquely put on our own lives. But friend, I'm here to tell you today that being divinely created is better than being earthly curated.

Being divinely created is better than being earthly curated.

I wonder, where do we find ourselves in the middle of this? Who, and what, are we allowing to influence us as a leader today? And even more importantly, how will we now lead in this generation with this noise?

Counterfeit Leadership

No wonder, then, we have such a strong fear that we are going to mess things up as leaders, because we are holding ourselves to an impossible standard. If we face this much pressure literally throughout our day as we scroll through our social media feeds, how much more will we put pressure on ourselves as leaders when all eyes are on us, and we carry our dream for many years?

As a society we are tired, weary, and quick to burn out. And as women leaders specifically we are not only facing the daily anxieties that come with media and culture around us, but our own unfair expectations. If we are not careful, **our drive to be perfect and live a perfectly curated life will lead us into a model of counterfeit leadership.**

Counterfeit leadership says, "I will show some of myself, but not the parts that I see as ugly or unworthy."

It insists, "I will curate, contrast, and control my narrative so that it will fit in the box of what I feel others demand or expect of me."

It demands, "I will be selective. I will edit myself and my public persona until I find the version that others deem worthy."

It teaches us that the minimum amount of effort required to just show up requires that we be consistently put together, not showing any cracks or weaknesses that would make us appear like a "bad" leader.

What's tricky is that on social media even our vulnerability is manufactured. Instagram might demand that we show vulnerability and give followers a window into our lives, and yet so many of us pick and choose what those pieces are. Some will show the corner of their messy bed, but not the rooms of clutter. They show the loving photo of their picture-perfect family, but not the fight they had right before the photo was taken. They will show a beaming selfie but not the tears poured out from feeling unworthy, leaving not just mascara streaks but a bruised and hurt ego. They will show the likes, comments, and highlights, but not the hours of comparison, self-judgment, and despair behind a blue checkmark. We will see the *completion* of their dream, but not the hard days when they wanted to give up and the grit that kept them going.

Even as I am writing this book today, it would be so easy to post pictures of myself typing away on a laptop in a cozy little cafe, but so much harder to show the half hour I had to talk myself into getting here in the first place because I wondered deep down if anyone would read a book I had written. If a blue checkmark, a community of followers, or a glossy, polished persona is what we are leading with in our leadership, we will always be left feeling empty because it's not what Jesus designed for us. We were really designed for connection.

Choosing What We See

This truth makes me think—what would have happened if the great leaders of the Bible had only shown us carefully curated profiles with their highlight reels?

We'd see the parting of the Red Sea but not the months in the desert and the manna of provision.

We'd see the prophecies of Daniel for Nebuchadnezzar but not how God saved him in the lion's den.

We'd see King David leading but not the decades he spent faithfully seeking and serving the Lord as a shepherd in the fields or his sin struggles that made him uniquely human. The Psalms wouldn't exist either.

We'd see Moses leading the masses with his staff, but not how he secretly asked God if he could choose his brother Aaron to take on the job instead of him.

We'd see the prodigal son living a lavish lifestyle in his father's home, but we'd never see his father's love and mercy poured out after he left and destroyed his own life.

We'd see Peter flawlessly leading the body of Christ but not the time he ran away from Jesus and denied him three times. Yet isn't this the very message that the prodigals of our generation need to hear—that they can still come back?

We'd see Thomas as a thriving leader but not the time he doubted—like we *all* do.

We'd see Jesus, the ascended Savior, but not the servant who sweated blood in Gethsemane, took on the weight of our sin, or who experienced all the struggles that we as humans face in our flesh on this side of heaven. We wouldn't know the same Jesus that understands betrayal and suffering, wept with Mary and Martha when Lazarus died, or the trials he overcame to show us the greatest depth of love, grace, and mercy the world has ever known.

The Lord's sacrifice would have been meaningless, and these leaders' endurance and resolve to pursue and see the Lord would all be erased. The comebacks, victories, and miracles that stir up our faith wouldn't be there anymore.

This is where we're at today, not just online but in our everyday lives. We've stopped allowing others to meet us in our vulnerability, mistakes, and need for God, and in turn we've stopped representing what the gospel really is. We've taken to sharing the mountaintop moments but not the time we spent ascending that made us builders in the process.

If I'm honest, my favorite people in the Bible are the ones who messed up in big ways because it makes me feel like I'm not the only one. I don't have perfect faith. I've drifted from my faith like Paul, doubted like Thomas. I've faced betrayal by friends and spiritual leaders I trusted. I've had days where I asked God to take away my calling just like Moses did because it felt like a burden I wasn't capable of carrying. I've even had some days where the I didn't want to follow Jesus at all anymore because the cost of it felt too high.

If we only show the highs and now the lows like these stories I just listed, we will most certainly...

- Feel alone, like we're the only ones.

- Feel defeated, like everyone else is doing better than us.

- Feel like we can never measure up, because frankly, we can't measure up to perfection.

- Feel like a failure before we start, *because with all this pressure who could even succeed to begin with?*

Making Sense of our Imperfections

Yet the gospel, the beautiful and life-giving gospel, offers us an entirely new perspective.

First, I believe that Jesus wants us to stop hiding. It so deeply pains the Father to see us editing and hiding pieces of ourselves that he so carefully and intentionally created. I think back to when the fires hit and one of my Instagram pages was designed for ministry, but I felt like I had to keep it perfectly curated and positive, so I didn't sound like a "downer" in front of my friends and work colleagues. And yet when I finally posted about it, so many people messaged me to ask how they could help and to share that they were so moved by what God was doing in the process. Have you ever done that, too, even subconsciously?

All of this reminds me of Adam and Eve, who hid. Yet Scripture tells us that those ugly, dark pieces, as well as the lighter, more lovely pieces, are all chosen by him. In the Psalms it is written: "How many are your works, Lord! In wisdom you made them all; the earth is full of your creatures" (Psalms 104: 24 - 25).

"First comes God's call and vision; then follows all the challenges and difficulties before you see the promise fulfilled."

God made each of us in wisdom and he saw this creation as good. I also love how David says it in Psalm 139:

> For you created my inmost being; you knit me together in my mother's womb. I praise you because I am fearfully and wonderfully made; your works are wonderful, I know that full well. My frame was not hidden from you when I was made in the secret place, when I was woven together in the depths of the earth. Your eyes saw my unformed body; all the days ordained for me were written in your book before one of them came to be. (Psalm 139:13 - 16)

Second, what the world truly needs is not a perfect leader, for that has already come in Jesus Christ. Our struggle for perfection is an insult to the Creator, who was perfect and created us in his perfect image. We weren't made for perfection but to display the righteousness of Christ. Scripture tells us that "God made him who had no sin to be sin for us, so that in him we might become the righteousness of God" (2 Corinthians 5:21).

Third, we need to learn that our vulnerability as leaders points others back to him. It is the fullness of who you are—in all of your vulnerability and even your mess—that makes you the leader the world needs. So many of us work ruthlessly to edit these pieces out of our curated stories. And yet, God is so inventive, so creative, that he has already factored in how he will use our greatest weaknesses and faults to tell the story of his glory. Friend, he sees the whole picture! What you see as a weakness, he sees as an opportunity for dependence and relationship with your Creator. It is an opportunity so share who we truly are.

Finally, I believe strongly that as followers of Jesus we have an obligation to closely observe and control what we allow to influence us. Jesus had only twelve close followers. And yet, he had influence and power in a way we could never imagine. Why do we feel that we need more?

The way of living like Jesus is the way of simplicity, a life lived with greater intention and less noise. If we are going to curate anything, don't spend that time on our profiles but on the influences around us. What kind of team and community around you will point you back to the way of Jesus? What music, TV shows, and films are you consuming, and how do you think they shape your thinking about the world? This might sound silly, but a few times a year I even scroll through the list of accounts on Instagram that I follow and I ask God if I should unfollow any of them. So start to ask God—what influences can I remove?

What we see as imperfect, God sees as divine design for our leadership. And in that place, he extends to us one of the greatest invitations we will ever receive: an opportunity to be fully known and fully loved as we come to value authenticity and vulnerability over having it all together.

What we see as imperfect, God sees as divine design for our leadership.

Now that we've learned how to face our self-doubt and stop comparing ourselves with others, we will talk about the next lie so many of us face when we finally step out and do what God has called us to do: imposter syndrome.

CHAPTER 7

Facing Imposter Syndrome

I first felt imposter syndrome when I started my foreign policy career in Washington, D.C. There were so many occasions where I was one of few women in the room, particularly in the national security space. In some meetings I was the *only* woman at our boardroom tables, surrounded by diplomats, generals, and leaders across the U.S. government.

One memory in particular stands out. I'll never forget when one morning as a freshly minted young professional my boss asked me to attend a think tank panel on nuclear security and report back with notes for our team. It was one of my first think tank events and I was wearing a brand-new pink top that I had just purchased the week prior. Pink is my favorite color, and I remember thinking that the bright pink color was so cheerful and upbeat during the dark winter months in D.C. Yet when I arrived at the event and looked out into a sea of black and charcoal grey men's suits as I tried to catch a glimpse of the speakers, I quickly realized I stood out like a sore thumb. While I already felt out of place as a woman and as one of the youngest people in the room, accidentally dressing like Elle Woods in Legally Blonde just put it over the edge. I made a quick mental note for future events.

Standing in that event in my pink shirt, I was facing *imposter syndrome* big time. I'd go on to face that same old foe dozens times more, like the time my boss had me stand in for him in a lunch with leaders of the World Bank only to—once again—be the youngest and the only woman, or the first time I was asked to speak in front of a big audience.

What I've learned is that so many of us get caught up in our own mind games that we take ourselves out of the game before it even starts, and the sad thing is we don't allow ourselves to truly enjoy the opportunities in front of us. We feel like we're both *too much* and *not enough*. We're not like that "other" leader in the room so there's no point in even trying. But aside from doubting our own abilities, talents, and appearance, we also doubt that we should be a leader in the first place. That we should even be at the table to begin with. I only wish I could go back and tell my young self to simply be present in those moments and really *own it*. The same is true when we have a big dream. Somewhere along the way we must learn to be our own biggest cheerleader. We have to remind ourselves that we actually do have a right to be there, and not only that but we have an important voice to share.

Try Anyway

The other secret I learned about imposter syndrome is that it affects so many more people than you'd think, even at the highest levels of leadership. Years after that "pink shirt" moment, I was a graduate student at Georgetown University and joined an intimate roundtable some female students had organized with the late Madeleine Albright, one of the most esteemed diplomats in American history, as a guest speaker. She was the first female to serve as the U.S. Ambassador to the United Nations, and in 1997 she served as the first female United States Secretary of State, paving the way for Condoleezza Rice and later Hilary Clinton to serve in the same office. Because of her contributions as woman in our field she had always been one of my biggest role models. In fact, for two years I even kept a copy of her memoir in my locker in case I ever ran into her on campus and could get her to sign it!

All the students in the room that day (including me!) wanted to ask her about—you guessed it—imposter syndrome. Secretary Albright shared how in her first days in office, she was overlooked because she was a woman. Leaders from traditional Middle Eastern countries even refused to meet with her until the President insisted on it. Can you imagine the implications of the United States not being included in these large international meetings? Yet as she grew in the role, she learned to overcome her feeling of imposter syndrome through research, extensive preparation, and an extra dose of courage. Later on, she also surrounded herself with other women and created cohorts that would support each other and magnify each other's voices to ensure they were heard in meetings. To Secretary Albright, the impact of their work far outweighed the social discomforts she experienced. She was there for a mission. And, as it turned out, being a woman was her greatest asset because she could speak into certain policy issues in ways that men couldn't. Of course, few of us will ever be appointed to a position of such magnitude (though I wouldn't say no!), but I believe the principle of what she shared holds true for all of us. Like her, *you deserve a seat at the table too.*

Her message reminded me that no matter what your position is, we all have moments where we feel out of place or like we don't belong. Can you imagine there are leaders who fly on Air Force One or have executive positions and still feel this way? And if we haven't yet, we most certainly will. There will always be moments we doubt. Try anyway! There may even be people who find ways to question our ability to lead because of our level of education, gender, or something else. Work towards it anyway. There will always be obstacles, and most often they're the negative voices in our own head telling us that we are not "enough." Try anyway.

Let Jesus Write the Story

I think back to the story of the Samaritan woman at the well, too, and how she felt like an outcast in her community. I imagine she had deep imposter syndrome. Because of Jesus, though, she suddenly had a sense of belonging and she was appointed by him to be a leader. She reminds me that although I feel intimidated or "not enough" in certain rooms or environments, if God has called me to be somewhere then I belong. Better yet, my qualifications to follow God's call on my life have nothing to do with my feelings and everything to do with the truth of the One who called me and created me in the first place. To me, this story is a story about an unexpected leader who encounters Jesus and finds her worth and her voice. The Samaritan woman didn't see herself as worthy, so she took herself out of the game. Same.

But here's the thing. If you remember any one thing about the Samaritan woman's story, it should be this: *Jesus still found her.* And not only that, he crossed a whole desert to get to her!

I can imagine Jesus walking through the dusty, scorching sand in the heat of the day as sweat dripped down his forehead. He took each step with determination because he knew he was about to radically change this woman's life and purpose. Everything in that picture just screams dedication. I really believe that he was willing to do whatever it took.

The greatest news about following Jesus is that he wants to do this for us too.

In our deepest feelings of inadequacy, Jesus daily pursues us. He offers us his grace so that we can live fully in all that he has for us. And in the same way that Jesus empowered the Samaritan woman at the well, he wants to light a fire in your heart as he calls you out to be a leader, too.

Let me encourage you today, friend, as he would. Jesus didn't send the most talented, brilliant, or accomplished people to carry out his mission. He's not looking for perfection, so neither should we. He promises that "his grace is sufficient" and that "his power would be made perfect in our weakness" (2 Corinthians 12:9).

We're all going to have moments where we feel like we're not enough to do what God is calling us to. But Jesus sees so much for you, and the story of the Samaritan woman proves that you haven't been disqualified. You are a vital piece of his mission to share the gospel around the world regardless of where you come from, what you've done, or what your circumstances may be.

Even more, your areas of deepest pain and unworthiness are a testimony that will shine his light into the world so others might see Jesus in their own pain.

Just like when I wore that pink shirt in a sea of black, let's agree to be imposters no more, because there's a world waiting for your gifts and your unique make up.

CHAPTER 8

You're Not the Main Thing

I know we just spent a chapter propping ourselves up a little bit in the face of imposter syndrome. But I think sometimes we also need the reminder that we're not the center of the story, or rather that we're living for a purpose far greater than ourselves. I know I need that.

I am convinced that what we need most today is a generation who is more focused on building an eternal legacy that will outlast finding fame on this earth. While I was writing this chapter, I came across an article on this topic that stopped me in my tracks. The author said:

> "Our families and churches desperately need leaders who will live for the welfare of days they'll never see." [5]

Here's my first question for you. **Are you so dedicated to Jesus that you will be willing to live for the welfare of days you will never, ever see?**

How does that make you feel? Does it make you uncomfortable, making you stir in your seat a little? Does it even feel a little bit unfair perhaps?

---

5 Hubbard, Scott. "Live for Days You Will Not See: The Beauty of Christian Legacy." *Desiring God*, 20 July 2023, www.desiringgod.org/articles/live-for-days-you-will-not-see. Accessed 18 July 2025.

I believe this question is at odds with an important part of our identity. Like we talked about in the last chapter, in our culture today we are constantly editing our own personal brands. We subconsciously market ourselves through our choices, big and small, online and offline. We desperately want to build a name for ourselves, with plenty of views, likes, and follows along the way. I would even go so far as to say that we think about ourselves and the appearance of having a neatly cultivated and curated life more than any generation before us. So putting our lives on the line for something that we will never even see the result of is counterintuitive to our human nature that is so geared toward promoting self.

We also love quick results—the faster, the better. Personally, I love that I can order something on Amazon Prime and it will come within hours, or an Uber driver will be at my curbside in minutes. Convenience and expediency are things we do so well, and they just make life so easy. The concept that we might pour our blood, sweat, and tears into our work to never see the full result or reward is so challenging, and yet this was the case for many of the disciples and our favorite Bible authors, like Paul. They built a church that they never saw the fruit of, and many of them, including Paul, were even beheaded before the church truly grew and expanded from the Mediterranean.

What Jesus is calling us to is entirely countercultural. He looks to a selfie generation and says, "What are you building for *me* that will outlast *you*?" And yet, as true disciples he is the life we must live. He is the brand we must carry and promote, not our own—*even if it means that we are working for the welfare of days we will never see.*

> **What Jesus is calling us to is entirely countercultural. He looks to a selfie generation and says, "What are you building for me that will outlast you?"**

Here's another tough question for you. The very same weekend that I gave my life to Jesus back in 2009, one of our conference speakers asked a question that I will never forget, and to this day it has marked my journey with the Lord.

The speaker, Patrick Fung, had put his life on the line to become a medical missionary who had spent decades in one of the countries that's most closed off from the gospel. He had gone through tremendous challenges and faced incredible risk to share Jesus with the many communities that their ministry reached across Asia. At the end of it all, you'd think he would have gotten dozens of awards or a standing ovation for his courage. But Dr. Fung followed a different path.

He exclaimed: "Some of the most important workers for the kingdom in the 21st century are the nameless people. They make Christ visible, not themselves."

Dr. Fung shared that his traditional Chinese family had instilled the values of stability and success, so to make them proud, he decided that he would become a doctor because it was seen as an honorable profession. But after giving his life to Christ during his first year of medical school, he changed course when he felt called to use his gifts on the mission field overseas, giving up any semblance of earthly "stability."

One day after he made this choice, he visited a library in London where he discovered dozens of names of missionaries just like him who had given their lives for the sake of the gospel in Southeast Asia. The thing is, he hadn't heard of one of them. He realized then that so many noble men and women before him had worked tirelessly and given their lives for Christ, **but they had lived to be forgotten so that Christ could become known.**

Let me ask you today, friend, how will your desire to magnify Christ supersede your desires to be known or be seen as successful or impressive? Are you ready to live to be forgotten, so that Jesus can get all the glory and his kingdom grow over ours?

Are you ready to give up your resume, your job titles, your comfort, your own desires for your life to follow his will above everything else?

In a world that seems more focused on gaining followers and blue check marks than living in anonymity, our challenge as disciples is to forsake it all as we take on God's call for our lives.

At the end of our days, our success as disciples will be measured strictly by our faithfulness and not by our popularity. Jesus didn't come for *impressive* leaders but for *humbled* leaders.

He is never going to ask us how many followers we have on social media or how many people listened to us as we spoke on a podium, but he *will* ask how we made disciples and brought the gospel to the ends of the earth. He'll ask us how we sacrificed and took risks of great faith to clothe the poor, care for the broken, and sit with the marginalized. We must remember that everything we have is from him, and so everything we have must be used for him too.

As we grow in influence, how can we make it less about us and more about Jesus? What would it look like if we spent less time working on our highlight reels and more time showing how are imperfections are met with his strength?

PART III

WHEN THE JOURNEY
GETS TESTED

CHAPTER 9

What Happens
When *Life* Happens?

We've talked about trusting God when he calls us and navigating comparison and self-doubt. These are all internal challenges, but what about the external obstacles that will inevitably arrive at our door?

A more straightforward way to say it is, *"What happens when life happens?"*

What's so interesting to me is that as we look at the stories of great leaders in the Bible we see this process is almost a rite of passage before we see the fruit of faithful, Kingdom-shaped leadership. Like Pastor Nicky Gumbel says, "First comes God's call and vision; then follows all the challenges and difficulties before you see the promise fulfilled." These seasons of refining—the hard, hidden, stretching ones—are so critical because it's where we learn to walk in deeper trust and greater holiness.

Earlier in the book I shared that my husband and I moved to Dallas right after we got married. That's when we walked through one of the hardest seasons in our lives. I wish I could say we walked around it—or had so much faith we just floated above it all—but that would be a disservice to you, reader, because that hasn't been our real journey as believers.

It all started like this: we were newly married, and God had powerfully called us to move to Dallas. He opened up positions for us both to serve in a ministry together. We filled our apartment with IKEA furniture and dreamed about all the amazing things that were in store for the next chapter. On the outside, we were picture-perfect newlyweds who had it all together. The world was laid out before us.

That's also our reality far surpassed our idealistic expectations. For the first year of our marriage, we had very little community. Yes, it was partially a product of moving to a new city, but I believe a major part of it was that Jesus wanted us to rely more closely on him as he started to refine us as leaders. I remember feeling so unseen and overlooked in this new environment. It was so far from what both of us had known.

We switched industries in our careers, working in ministry for the very first time. I struggled with missing the policy work in Washington, D.C., and my husband Chad missed being in the epicenter of the entertainment industry in Los Angeles.

Then, we walked with loved ones through health issues, and I experienced the loss of four family members in two months. We experienced profound betrayal by multiple people we had trusted and deeply admired. Hurt by other Christians, no Christian leader seemed trustworthy.

We worked through relational strain as unprocessed pain, trauma, and brokenness surfaced in our lives. Then, during so much stress, we experienced new and unprecedented physical ailments as migraines, stomachaches, insomnia, physical exhaustion, and adrenal fatigue took their toll.

If you were a fly on the wall in this season, you would see that we navigated loneliness, financial stress, anxiety, spiritual attacks, disappointment, unprecedented delay, and pressure that crushed us to the core.

I had mountaintop moments followed quickly by moments of fear where I questioned God's love and why this was all happening. I questioned why bad things happened to good people. I'll be honest, I had days where I secretly wondered if he was truly good—how could we follow him in faithfulness and then experience this kind of crisis? Looking back, I know I struggled to share those things with friends because I wanted to look like I had it all together.

Yet as we faced what felt like a cloud of unrelenting obstacles, we would catch glimpses of the sweetness of life. Friends had babies after miscarriages, years of delay, and unexplained infertility. We even saw a miracle baby for a friend who was told she could never carry her own children. We saw relationships struggle, but we also saw weddings and married couples reunited after infidelity. We saw prodigals walk back into church with us. We saw countless miracles over our finances, health, and practical circumstances. We met people who prayed over us and saw once strangers become our dearest friends, friends who carried their own scars too.

It was the hardest season I have ever gone through, but when I look back, I would do it all again for the woman of God it has made me. Because we were broken down so much, we had to turn to Jesus with a new level of desperation and need. Going through the motions as a successful leader in a suit and heels just wasn't going to cut it anymore.

I pray my story can remind and encourage you today that there is so much purpose in these hard seasons in life. As leaders we often look at big numbers to measure our success but personally, it's in these seasons of hiddenness and struggle where I realize I truly became a leader. I rejoice in sharing that God used it to change me from the inside out into the woman he had created me to be, shredding my pride, my distractions, and anything else that kept my gaze from him. And I can rejoice in sharing with you, dear reader, that if you're going through it right now, the best has just begun.

All that to say, life definitely happened. But *life* also happened, meaning Jesus brought life out of a season that felt like death all around me.

Perhaps you are in this season now, or maybe it's years ahead of you. Either way, my message is the same. Don't run from it. Embrace it as a time of formation and a training season for greatness. If I could go back to myself at that time, here are the top four things I would say to do.

1.) Take note of times when the Lord was faithful and good. Remember his miracles in his life and take time to thank him.

2.) Spend time with God in worship.

3.) Intentionally ask God where he was and is in the difficult places.

4.) Talk to someone about your questions. Surround yourself with people whose faith you admire and be vulnerable enough to let them carry you through.

Last, I want to pray with you. Being a Christian isn't about just getting up and saying God is good every time something bad happens. That's a beautiful response, but if it's not real or genuine we can put it aside until we really believe it to be true.

Lord, I thank you that you are not afraid of our pain or the darkness in the world, but you come even closer to us when we are suffering or brokenhearted. I thank you that you showed us what love is by coming to us, making the first move, and making a way for us to have true intimacy and relationship with the Father. Help me in this season to feel your presence and love in a new way. When I feel discouraged, give me eyes to see the story you are writing for my life instead of only seeing the challenges before me. On days when I feel hopeless, give me strength and your peace that surpasses all understanding. Jesus, I give you every difficult situation I am facing, and I pray you would reveal to me how you are working it all for my good. Even if I can't see the full picture right now, I choose to put my trust and faith in you today. I submit it all to you, my Savior.

A Letter for Your Discouragement

Dear Reader,

I wrote this letter in a time of discouragement with the hopes that it will encourage you, too, on days when you face disappointment, opposition, and what feels like limitless days of waiting.

As you begin to walk in all that God has called you to, you're going to start facing a lot of opposition.

There is a spiritual enemy who doesn't want you to succeed.

Sometimes we're our own enemy, caught in a self-destructive cycle of self-doubt. When I wrote this book and launched my nonprofit, my greatest fear was, *Can I do it?*

As we've unpacked in this book and look through stories in Scripture, the answer is no. Actually, its a *hard no.* Eventually, every leader will reach the limit of their own abilities. But God can, and he can do above and beyond what we ask or think.

Finally, there are real and tangible people around you who aren't going to understand it. In my own life, that's included the people I love and trust the most.

The only ones who will truly understand what you're doing, what you're walking through now, and what you're called to are you and God. That's a lonely truth to recognize but we can also find tremendous power from it. The very one who knit you in your mother's womb, who conquered death, and who created you has you now.

We can't look outside without seeing his glory on display around us. It's a tangible reminder of his faithfulness and incredible love for us.

So, friend, I urge you to press into his embrace. Put your head up, roll your shoulders back, and watch him do tremendous, miraculous, life-changing, kingdom-shaking things through you. God uses broken vessels to make beauty, even out of our greatest mistakes and sin.

Rest in him and watch the potter create something new in and through you.

One last thing—there is *joy* on the other side of this journey. It feels like pressing in to him is too much some days, or that the thing he's asked is too big. But know that there's joy, breakthrough, and deep purpose.

When we partner with Jesus, we're partnering with heaven, and we get to experience it through him as we do his work in this earthly place.

Cheering you on,
Amy

CHAPTER 10

Through the Tunnel

The thing about suffering is that nobody wants it, we often avoid it, and we rarely can anticipate it. It feels so overwhelming and so painful, that it's the last place we want to be. Even though we all face hard seasons in some way or another, suffering is one of those topics that we so often rush through in church culture, especially here in the United States. It makes sense—our avoidance of suffering is frankly normalized in American culture today. But, at what cost to our *souls*?

Once a pastor from Kenya joined us on Sunday at our church in Washington D.C. He told us the story of his first visit to Target. He shared that he was amazed at the selection and variety of things he could get all in this one place. Then he turned and said, "In Kenya, suffering is a part of life. In America, you have so much. The aisles at Target were so full, you have so many options! Can you believe it? An entire store, filled with things to avoid suffering!"

Wow, isn't he right? From medication to quick fix items, there are so many ways we try to work our way around suffering. We want everything in our life at our fingertips, when we want it.

If we're really honest, I think we see suffering as part of life, and yet we deeply fear that if we faced it head-on, we wouldn't be able to handle it. Once we open that Pandora's box, we fear we won't be able to stop the bleeding that suffering brings—and then what? What will we be left with? If we really face our sorrow, our grief, our loss, our weakness head-on, how will we recover? Isn't it better to skip over it or move on?

Or perhaps we do sometimes approach suffering ourselves, but we fear inviting God into it with us. We wonder, *"What do I do with my faith if God disappoints me?"* It can feel at times like he's left us behind.

Even as Christians who have been around church for a long time, many of us lack the tools to excavate our suffering well, and that's fair because we weren't meant to do it alone. We need to be taught, led, and instructed by others who have experienced freedom and lead us through it. Suffering is never welcome and there is never a good time for it. But the truth is, in life it can't be avoided, and it often follows us exactly where we are until we learn from it.

So what do we do with our suffering? I once organized an interview with a woman named Joni Eareckson Tada to capture the story of her life. If you aren't familiar with her journey, she had an accident at the age of seventeen that left her paralyzed from the neck down. She went on to become an incredible leader that has changed millions of lives around the world. She even wrote over forty books, recorded several musical albums, starred in an autobiographical movie of her life, and became an artist. Joni also is the founder of Joni and Friends, an organization that ministers to the disability community.

Yet what is most impressionable to me is her contagious joy and the sweetest, most beautiful relationship she has with Jesus. She shared how after years of being so angry at God for her injury, even attempting suicide multiple times, Jesus changed her perspective and softened her heart to make her a leader.

Where we see our greatest pain, Jesus often has an invitation for us to encounter him and to be made anew in Christ.

Then, she looked right into the camera said definitively, "I think God allows what He hates to accomplish what he loves."

Where we see our greatest pain, Jesus often has an invitation for us to encounter him and to be made anew in Christ.

Let It Build You

The Celtics tradition talks about something called a "thin place," sacred places in life where heaven is closest to earth. To me, suffering is one of those places. It's in our suffering, not just in the highs of life, that we experience the presence of Jesus most closely. He knew suffering so well because he lived through it himself and even died on the cross.

So if you are going to suffer, let it build you. Let it guide you into the comfort of experiencing the deep love of your Heavenly Father. Let it develop and permeate into your character until you are made anew. Let it be the place where you courageously accept the call of your Lord and Savior into deeper healing and freedom.

I love this question that author and pastor Tyler Stanton asks about suffering in his book *Praying Like Monks, Living Like Fools* after sharing about his own journey through suffering while battling stomach cancer. He asks, "Will the pain, suffering, and needs that intrude on our own stories harden our hearts, or will they soften our souls? How does the very pain that is eating us alive become an agent of deep transformation? We have to invite God—the very One who broke our trust—into the muck with us. We invite the One we are labeling "perpetrator" to be our healer. It's the most courageous of all choices." [6] Inviting Jesus into our suffering is the bravest thing we'll ever do.

Here's one more way to look at it. A friend once told me that addressing our suffering alone without Jesus—the collection of

---

6 Staton, Tyler. 2022. *Praying like Monks, Living like Fools*. Zondervan.

our past hurts, pains, big "T" traumas and little "t" traumas—feels something like entering a dark cave. Most of us know the cave is there but we dress it up to make it a little more tolerable. Maybe we add some nice furniture, mood lighting, and a new rug. We come in and out, but we mostly stay out of there if we can help it. Many people we encounter in life will choose to sweep past pain under the rug their entire lives as they look to find meaning in the world around them, like work, school, or relationships, until it accumulates and eventually becomes unbearable. The problem is that these things will never satisfy us or give us the love, joy or purpose we all crave.

On the other hand, my friend said, when we enter the cave with Jesus, it becomes more like a tunnel. Imagine a dark space that Jesus illuminates with a flashlight, guiding us through our hurts and then bringing us back out the other side into the most beautiful sunny, green pasture you've ever seen. This is a picture of the famous Scripture in Psalm 23: "Even though I walk through the darkest valley, I will fear no evil, for *you are with me (emphasis added)*, your rod and your staff, they comfort me" (Psalm 23:4). Jesus is at the end of the tunnel of our suffering, standing in the light, ready to show us a way out and into freedom. Only the Creator who created our hearts can truly mend them.

Let It Change You

Jesus' heart is not for us to simply sit in our pain, but ultimately to walk through it with him and find a deeper healing. Our relationship with him isn't just about a future promise of salvation, but about finding him in the here and now. Christ, who knows suffering intimately, invites us to co-suffer with Him, trusting that resurrection life awaits. It is the Father's tender love that transforms us from the inside out, enabling us to lead others with a changed heart.

So this is our charge: we can spend our lives being Christians who memorize Scripture, show up every Sunday, and serve others, but if we do not taste this fullness of the freedom, peace, and joy that Christ is offering in the here and now and especially in our hardest moments, we are missing the point. I wholeheartedly believe that it is not enough to merely "know" about the resurrection life in our minds but to have a transformative encounter with a living God who tenderly and powerfully meets us beyond our head knowledge in the deepest parts of our souls.

Suffering means facing our pain, and yet it yields necessary fruit that is absolutely pivotal to Kingdom leadership: intimacy with Jesus. It's where the information stored in our head makes its longest journey twelve inches south to our hearts, where we become transformed disciples of Christ. It's not lost on me that Jesus suffered on the cross from betrayal, rejection, and physical agony. Suffering is an intimate part of the gospel story. We can reject suffering, or in it we can see the cup of life that Jesus took and the resurrection life that came from it. Suffering feels like a taste of death here on earth, and yet our co-suffering with Christ is what brings the purpose and life our souls have been longing for all along. This is ultimately where our greatest and deepest leadership formation often begins.

Next time you suffer, what will your response be? Will you run from Jesus, or commit to encountering him in the darkness? Will you accept his great invitation? If we have to suffer in life, let it build us into great leaders.

If we have to suffer in life, let it build us into great leaders.

CHAPTER 11

Pick Up Your Mat

Jesus sees and understands our emotions as we bring our challenges and hard seasons to him. He empathizes with them and grieves alongside us. But he doesn't want us to stay there. He loves us enough to not to let our pain become our identity. Ultimately, I believe he is on a mission to not only free us but empower us to bring others into freedom, just like he did for the Samaritan woman and in my own story.

John 5 tells the story of a man who learned this lesson in a powerful way. This man had been struggling for a long time, thirty-eight years to be exact. That's a long time! During that time, you could have seen thirty-eight different Superbowl championships and nine Olympics. It's an eternity. And during all of that, this man had been exiled, singled out, and alone.

And yet, Jesus came to him. That's where he chose to be on this particular day—at the pool of healing, not at a feast, not with his friends or family. With the blind and lame, the paralyzed, he felt at home. Though this man had suffered like we all do, Jesus healed him. This is such a beautiful picture and reminder for all of us walking through healing of what is possible in Christ!

Some time later, Jesus went up to Jerusalem for
one of the Jewish festivals. Now there is in Jerusalem near the Sheep Gate a pool, which in Aramaic
is called Bethesda and which is surrounded by five
covered colonnades. Here a great number of dis-
abled people used to lie—the blind, the lame, the
paralyzed. One who was there had been an inval-
id for thirty-eight years. Jesus saw him lying there
and learned that he had been in this condition for
a long time.... (John 5:1-3)

Whether you have faced a physical ailment or not, isn't this
true of life? Disappointment? Betrayal? Abandonment? Break-
ups? Divorce? Waiting with unanswered prayers? We all have places where our heart is a little sick. And in that place, resentment and
impatience grow and hope wanes.

Sometimes, if it goes long enough, we give up altogether.
That hopelessness is something we are all bound to face one way
or another. I know I faced that several times when we were going
through that difficult season in Dallas. So when Jesus asks him this
next question, I can just imagine there's doubt and so much pain
in his heart.

Jesus stops in his tracks, looks at this man, and asks him, "Do
you want to get well?"

Wow. Do you want to get well is a very loaded question. First
of all, this is Jesus. He's probably followed by dozens of men and
women. All eyes are on this guy, and now everyone's looking at
him. If you were him, what would you say back?

I bet if he had asked this man years ago—decades ago—he
would have said an emphatic yes! I want to get well! Heal my body!
I'm ready for my breakthrough! I'm ready for healing! Pick me! I
want to get well! I want to sing, dance, and skip! I want to live!

But then *life* happened to him and healing started to feel so far away. I wonder what went through this man's head when Jesus asked him, "Do you want to get well?" He was skeptical. He believed Jesus was just another person offering him empty promises. He was like the rest of them. So many people had offered him healing but they didn't deliver. Maybe he thought Jesus was crazy. This man whom he'd never seen before believes he is a healer? Who is this guy? Why should I trust him? I've heard all about him but who is he really? So then this man looks up and replies:

> "'Sir, I have no one to help me into the pool when the water is stirred. While I am trying to get in, someone else goes down ahead of me'" (John 5:7).

Have you ever felt like you wanted and *needed* breakthrough down to the core of your being, but every time you look up it feels like everyone else is getting it but you? They got their financial breakthrough. They have a blessed marriage. They have perfect kids. They're able to have children in the first place. She found healing. *He* got promoted?!

And as everyone passes us by with their answered prayers, we say inside, "They all just seem so happy . . . and yet here I am in this mess."

Down to your core, we desire it more than anything else even though you may not have the courage to admit it out loud, but— there's a but. It's like that's for everyone else but me.

I want to speak to that for a second. There's a bruise that may be bigger than what you can see. The odds seem stacked against you.

I wonder if that's a taste of how this man felt. Thirty-eight years is a long time. And we see that he didn't even ask for healing at this point—he had given up. He felt like he was down on his luck and there weren't any breakthroughs left for him.

In the midst of it all, when everyone else's prayers are being answered but yours, would you believe that Jesus wants that healing for *you*? I know I've been there.

Despite the buts and the "not me"s, Jesus breaks the tension. Then Jesus said to him, "Get up! Pick up your mat and walk."

Nobody saw this coming. Not even him! This man has been sitting on his mat for nearly four decades. Maybe he used to know how to walk, maybe not at all. And then there's this mat. His mat that he's been sitting on for all these years? It's totally soiled. It's caked in mud and dirt. It's been covered in sweat. They don't have laundromats for mats like his. The edges are coming apart, the top of it is scuffed as he turns on it to find a comfortable position. And the profound thing is that in many ways, it looks like his heart on the inside—worn down.

You see, to this man, the distance between this mat on the ground and the eyes of Jesus' feet above felt like the Grand Canyon. Because it was layered in all the nos. It's layered in years of desperation and hopelessness. It's made even further by the people who treated him as less than because of his condition. They looked down on him—all his life.

"How could this man, this random man who just walked up to me, do this? Isn't he like *them* who look down at me? Why does he look at me differently?"

And then, his heart starts to give way as he looks at Jesus with his eyes burning in compassion. He doesn't look at me like they did. Something is different.

His heart skips a beat. Is this someone who doesn't look down on me, but maybe he's the first person to finally look AT me? Does he see ME? Is he the first person who really sees me?

So he does something he's never done. There have been a million nos. There have been so many attempts to heal. Day by day, he sat in agony waiting, but he decided he would try one last time.

And he did the bravest thing he'd ever done. He got up. Scripture says, "At once the man was cured; he picked up his mat and walked" (John 5:9).

This is big. This is monumental. A hush fell over the crowd. Any eye that was looking away was now surely looking at him. But it was different. They weren't not looking down at him. They were seeing him for the first time. He was standing! He was walking! And he picked up his mat. His mat is now more than the home of his despair.

In this moment, his life changed. All the doubt, the disappointment, the hopelessness, wondering when healing would come melted away.

His mat became the trophy of what Jesus had done. He was the one he could finally put his trust in. He was the one who promised and finally delivered. He was the one who saw him for who he truly was.

The heavens rejoiced. The angels cried! This man had been set free. And not just because he could stand. Not just because he could walk. But because he picked up the mat of his shame, his loneliness, his place of deepest despair, and he moved through Jesus. And the past? It didn't just melt away. These patches of dirt on his mat, the roughness of its texture, the rips, the tears . . . they were battle scars. Isn't it interesting that even our Savior still has the scars in his hands? He's not afraid of your pain.

Where are you wanting a breakthrough? What has plagued you? Depression? Anxiety? Addiction? Is it a physical ailment? What's your mat? I've held many mats of my own: loneliness in friendships, anxiety, an autoimmune disorder, betrayal and hurt in relationships, comparison, and more. I get it.

Jesus said to this man on the mat—and he says to us today— just trust me. Do it one more time. This time, it's different. Because the power and presence of Jesus—Healer, Messiah, King of Kings—is before you. But you're going to have to *believe* first.

Jesus was on a mission. He wasn't going to let anything get in the way of what he was doing or about to do. And that is the case for us. If we seek him, if we just give him that last dose of hope, just look at what he can do.

So today, stand up. Take account of your bruises and wounds, all of the no's and the rejection that left you on the ground. As we look into the eyes of Jesus, our faith grows. Come, pick up your mat. Accept the healing and freedom Jesus offers you to no longer let your pain define you as a victim but as a victor in Christ. And walk. As you do, look around you—all of the others walking with you too, a great crowd of witnesses. *And heaven will cheer.*

PART IV

HITTING THE WALL

CHAPTER 12

Let's Check In

Did you know that only 1% of the population will complete a marathon in their lifetime?

Growing up, my father started volunteering as a coach for his running club in LA. Week after week, thousands of runners would meet for a training run by the beach as the sun came up.

Often people would start the season in this club with no running experience at all. They'd hardly be able to run one mile that first week, never mind 26.2! Some people are even overcoming injuries or have lost weight just to be able to run at all.

The whole point of this club was yes, to get people out running more, but it was largely to train everyone for the LA Marathon. To get ready, the runners would run routes that increase in distance each week. They'd stretch, strength train, hydrate, and wear the best shoes that would help them keep up their running game. And yet, despite *all* that training and preparation, scientists have proven that every single runner faces a wall at some point in the race where they run out of fuel.

Most people say that runners hit this point in the race—informally called *the wall*—somewhere around 18 to 20 miles. At this moment, glycogen stores are lower as the body tries to use every ounce of energy it can, so runners start to tire out. The wall is reflected by real physiological process. Still, accompanied by a *mental* and even an *emotional* wall, runners feel like they can't keep going to finish their race. As the body tires, the mind says it's time to stop or give up altogether. The lure of a rest break, a nap, or maybe a juicy cheeseburger becomes much more real than it seemed at the start line!

What's crazier is that this wall is completely inevitable, even for the world's most experienced marathon runners and Olympic competitors!

Running the Race

At some point in our spiritual race to live out God's call for our lives, we all get tired, too. And just like running a physical race and encountering the "wall" doesn't happen by accident, we have to prepare for the roadblocks and challenges that may occur as we pursue God's plan and purpose for our lives. As humans, we simply have limits. You better believe after that season in Dallas, I had reached my limit.

We might start with deep passion, vigor, and energy, but in a longer race, we will tire. We *will* grow weak. And, inevitably, as our energy wanes, we often want to give up, even if that's totally different from our plan when we first started. This is the point where many people give up on their faith altogether.

We will *all* have moments of wanting to give up at some point in our lives, and that's why these next few chapters teach us not only to *expect* this wall, but also *how to prepare for it.*

This is the story of almost every great leader we see in the Bible, too. They *all* hit walls. From Moses to Abraham, each one was called to a monumental purpose, only to face major obstacles they didn't expect when they set out. Therefore, like runners training for a marathon, we, too, as believers, need to train and plan for the challenges we will face on this side of Heaven as we pursue our dreams with full force.

How do we stay the course when life gets hard and not give up altogether? We stay rooted in the principles that Jesus lived by, and we'll discuss several of them in this section.

So far, this book has involved a lot of introspection as we've looked at topics like comparison, self-doubt, and imposter syndrome. We've also addressed what happens when our journey is tested and what we do with our pain.

Hang with me in this section as we do one last heart check-in and then move on to some practical tips for our everyday lives. Consider this section your own personal toolkit you can refer back to whenever you need it.

How's Your Heart?

Did you know that the most vital question you'll ever ask of yourself as a leader has nothing to do with the ways most of us measure our impact at work? This question has nothing to do with your revenues, quarterly reporting, or how you manage team dynamics. It's also probably something you don't often get asked about on the street, at Thanksgiving dinner with your relatives, or even with your closest friends.

Here it is. *How is your heart doing today?*

Stay with me. I don't mean it in a super hokey way. I don't mean it flippantly either. Not just a quick "How are you doing" you ask of a coworker in the office, to which you would likely shrug and say, "Everything 's good!"

Maybe you even say with some gusto, "I'm doing *great!*"

But of course, we all know most of us aren't "*great*" all the time. So I want to get real and vulnerable with you. This is a safe place after all.

I mean this: Friend, how is your heart *doing?* How are you *really?* When it's just you, when all the distractions are taken away and the business of your day quiets down, how are you really doing?

If you're like me, you probably don't love that question and it might even make you pause for a moment. In my experience, people either feel like that question is too cheesy, or even more so, they wince at the idea of opening a Pandora's box of mixed emotions. I mean, who wants to unpack the baggage in our lives when we can just look at the box instead?

The other problem is that once we start unpacking the box, we don't know how to stop. So instead of facing it, we just try to look more put together. That's how we feel most leaders should be, right? Responsible, in charge, confident? We make it this beautiful package on the table with satin ribbon and gorgeous wrapping paper, fit for Martha Stewart herself. If it's going to be there, maybe we can just make it better looking.

The problem is that we have to unpack the box eventually, or it will break us. And if that's not reason enough for us, it will negatively affect the very people we're leading and trying to love well in our lives—our spouse, our kids, our friends. The sad truth is that it often hurts the people we want to protect the most. It's essential to our leadership.

So friend, let me ask you again. How is your heart doing?

Now, the real reason that your answer might be "not great" is because the data reveals that is actually the case, statistically, for most people. According to Boston College, rates of anxiety and depression in US adults between the ages of 18 and 29 increased to 65 and 61 percent during the COVID pandemic. 7The Pew Research Center confirms that these numbers remained high through late 2022. Levels of psychological distress have fluctuated for many respondents since then, but many of them reported that

---

7 Hayward, Ed. 2021. "COVID-19'S Toll on Mental Health." Www.bc.edu. April 2021. https://www.bc.edu/bc-web/bcnews/campus-community/faculty/anxiety-and-stress-spike-during-pandemic.html.

they still felt hopeful about the future very little of the time (one to two days per week). At least some of the time during the week they also had trouble sleeping (64%); felt nervous, anxious or on edge (61%); felt depressed (46%) or lonely (42%). 8

Your pastors, the ones we look up to and who always seem so strong? They're feeling it too. According to Boston University, approximately 38% of US pastors considered quitting ministry altogether in 2021. That's almost *half*!

These numbers are at historical highs, and to this day the mental health community continues to examine the full psychological impact of the pandemic. At the very least, we can clearly state that there has been a significant toll on our emotional, mental, and spiritual health and it's going to take a while to sort through it all.

All of these external pressures merely add to many of the pain points that were already present in the church before the pandemic. Here are a few:

1.) Anxiety

2.) Comparison

3.) Hidden sin struggles

4.) Self-harm

5.) Addiction

6.) Depression

7.) Unprocessed childhood trauma

8.) Health struggles

9.) Church hurt

10.) Family strife

---

8 Gramlich, John. 2023. "Mental Health and the Pandemic: What U.S. Surveys Have Found." Pew Research Center. Pew Research Center. March 2, 2023. https://www.pewresearch.org/short-reads/2023/03/02/mental-health-and-the-pandemic-what-u-s-surveys-have-found/.

If you associate with any of these, know that you are not in the minority. We all have different areas of struggle. If your heart is not at its best, you are in good company. So let's talk, then, about what we can do about it.

Daily Rhythms of Rest

Next, I want to walk through how we can reshape our daily practices to honor God. Let's start with a little personal inventory. As you go through the list below, mark a number next to each line. 0 = Never, 1 = Sometimes, and 2 = Almost Always. At the end, take a total and see what your final number is.

_____ When you wake up, you spend time with God first before picking up your phone.

_____ You take at least fifteen minutes daily to pause and rest without screens.

_____ When you physically reset, you also rest emotionally and mentally (not ruminating on the past, making lists, or planning for the future).

_____ You set boundaries around your time. Nos to social engagements are said with love and clarity.

_____ You set parameters around how much time you spend on social media.

_____ You set parameters around how much time you spend on your phone.

_____ You take a full Sabbath day once a week.

_____ You have meaningful conversations with mentors or friends in your inner circle once a month.

_____ You have sat with a professional to thoroughly talk through past pain, including trauma or abuse.

_____ You have a "safe space" you can go to in order to fully decompress when you need to reset.

All finished? Now, add up your total.

If your final score was over 16, you're doing a great job finding rhythms of rest. Now, look through the list to examine which numbers were lowest. If there were any that were marked as "0," note them and commit yourself to changing one every other week. Where can you make space to build new rhythms?

If your final score was 15 or under, you're still growing in finding your rhythms. Look through the list and highlight any numbers that you marked as "0." Take note of each of them and try to commit yourself to changing one every other week.

If these life rhythms are something you struggle with, I strongly encourage you to check out The Rule of Life system that was developed by Stephen Macchia. Developing a personal rule of life helps us to establish our schedules with a set of guidelines and commitments. It focuses on three areas: being with Jesus, becoming like Jesus, and doing what Jesus did. John Mark Comer's books Practicing the Way and The Ruthless Elimination of Hurry are also great options that have been an encouragement to me.

Finding Our Rest in Jesus

If you associated with anything in the section above, I want to offer you some helpful resources. If we're all feeling it—the restlessness, the tiredness, the *grind* of just surviving. It's normal, it's okay, and there's help.

First, I want to encourage you with the rest that Jesus has for you. You are deeply and overwhelmingly loved by your Heavenly Father. He's promised us, "In this world you will have trouble. But take heart! I have overcome the world" (John 16:33).

I also want to remind you that he's already come and died for us so that we would have peace. It's not something that we need to desperately strive or fight for. Instead, our job is to claim his peace and live it out in our everyday life. Remember that marathon story I shared earlier? The "walls" we all hit in life have a lot to do with a lack of rest.

This week, start by setting aside some time to sit at his feet. Rather than racing to get through your day, I challenge you to take twenty minutes to simply worship and rest in his presence. Let your soul be replenished by the Father and see what delights he has in store for you. It's the very thing our hearts were designed to do. We will all face the inevitable wall at some point. But it's often the counter-intuitive rhythms of rest that will help us push through.

CHAPTER 13

Opting In

Let's jump into the next practice that will strengthen us to become leaders who can go the distance: inviting the Holy Spirit into our lives. After God called me to start The Well Initiative, I spent a long time feeling overwhelmed. As an entrepreneur, I would have to learn new skills from scratch. On the most basic level, there were so many small steps to laying the foundations of my nonprofit, like learning how to legally set it up, build a website, fundraise, and open a bank account. But behind it all, there was a much deeper challenge: realigning my identity from the career I had known, where I could work quietly behind the scenes, to now being thrown into the spotlight as the founder. Honestly, many of those days I wanted to give up on my dream altogether.

You could say I was hitting some walls.

Then one day, something clicked. I was interviewing someone I deeply admired as a businesswoman and as a believer. Her name is Alisa Keeton and she is the founder of Revelation Wellness, a nonprofit ministry dedicated to educating and inspiring others to live healthy and whole in Christ. She's also a bestselling author and amazing podcast host, and I've admired her for years.

So when I finally got a chance to talk to her one-on-one, I knew exactly what to ask her.

"Alisa, did you also feel weary or afraid in your leadership journey?"

Even as the question flew out of my mouth I was secretly wondering, *Am I the only one who's trying to run from their dream? What's wrong with me, God?"*

With tremendous grace and compassion, she told me that she had struggled with her call too. She had even laughed the first time a friend called out her giftings and suggested she should start her own company!

My heart started warming up to her and my shoulders fell a few inches down my back. I let out a big exhale. Maybe I wasn't the only one?

I shuddered as she told me she had tried to run away too—like Jonah, like *me!*—until God finally told her that he was going to accomplish his purposes with or without her.

Like a girl whose father was leaving to go to war, she said, she decided to go with God into the battle.

Alisa shared that God wasn't going to withdraw the call over her life. That same call would be there for her whole life, but she had to decide if she would opt into it. She had to decide if she was going to surrender and open the door to let God in. I knew in that moment that I had already been set by God, but I needed to choose to opt in and open the door where he had been knocking for so long.

Her response was an answer to prayer for me. Here was this woman I so admired, and I realized for the first time I wasn't the only one. If you're reading this, maybe you've felt the same way! I pray you would be encouraged the same way I was that day.

If this conversation wasn't already lighting enough fire beneath me, there was one last sucker punch. At the end of the call, Alisa offhandedly shared that now, decades later, she gets emails all the time from women who shared that God had called them to do the same thing years ago, but they were too afraid to do it! Yikes!

Today, Alisa is on *Good Morning America*, interviewing incredible leaders like Beth Moore and so many of my favorite Christian leaders, and her books have made a life-changing impact.

That night, I couldn't stop thinking about our conversation. What was the "secret" that kept her going that I wasn't tapping into? She could have said no to the call of God in her life, but she eventually changed her mind. She was *doing* the thing, and not only that, she was thriving! She was leading tens of thousands of women into freedom with her, including me. The light from the glow of Christ within her had reached me, way across the country. That is just what I wanted for myself and what I had longed for all along, but I had just felt too weak to get there.

As I thought about what made Alisa different from all those other women, who had also been called but said no, she had her opt-in moment. She made a choice every day to keep at it, even when it was hard. I realized that if I was going to succeed in my own God-given destiny, I was going to have to choose to opt in every day. I would have to do the very thing I was afraid to do and just do it afraid until it started flowing naturally. And a lot of that had to do with simply overcoming my own self-doubt.

I was also going to have to rely on the Holy Spirit and the presence of God. Fear hadn't been removed from Alisa's life, but it had been extinguished by the incredible joy and delight she had in her Heavenly Father.

"The presence of God," she said, "is what you need the most! Not just going to church, or even praying, but daily and earnestly seeking the very presence of God and the Holy Spirit to enliven us, strengthen us, and embolden us to do what no human alone can do."

So that is the story behind the opt-in. Now let's talk about how we put gasoline on the fire in our souls: we invite the Holy Spirit in. The Bible tells us that Christ lived a perfect life and died for our sins. When he rose again, he gave us a tool called the Holy Spirit.

A Story of Two Pictures

As I processed this conversation with Alisa, God gave me a picture that perfectly demonstrates why inviting the Holy Spirit is so crucial to our journey.

Imagine with me that you see a picture of two different bikes riding in completely different terrain. (Now, I'm probably the last person who should be talking about bike metaphors. True story, when I was eight, I crashed my bike in a sandy patch on a hill and knocked my front tooth out. To this day my front tooth is patched up and it took me years to get on a bike again, but I love it now!)

The first is a racing bike with two wheels. This bike is racing up a rocky, dirt path going up a mountain at full speed. If you've ever seen cyclists racing in the Olympics, it looks something like that. It's an athletic, all-in sprint that uses every ounce of energy left in your muscles. You're riding the bike up this hill as dust and rocks fly at your face and sweat drips down your forehead.

This image, God said, represents the hamster wheel of trying to keep up with everyone else around you. This is a picture of the hustle. The grind. This is what the hill to become that "girl boss" feels like. It's where we try to be the best and the most successful. It's where we want to have the cutest, nicest outfit in the room, the designer handbag, the Pinterest-worthy house, the fancy vacation, the Christmas-card worthy family, all the things. It's where our flesh brings us daily, our Instagram feeds scroll to . . . and it's also where we are at last wiped clean of all we've got within ourselves. It's where we spend all our time looking around to accrue the things that will finally make us enough, but we can hardly look at ourselves in the mirror because we've out-compared ourselves to everyone else.

What we don't see in the hustle and grind is that it's an uphill battle and the top of the hill keeps moving. This happens not just in the world but in ministry too. There's no end in sight and our culture today will tell us go and go and go until we face burnout and eventually stop.

Okay, so that's the first picture. Do you feel the stress and pressure of the hustle in your bones as you're imagining it? Do you feel how that threshold keeps getting higher and higher, wider and wider? Do you see how we keep adding more checklist items to the secret little bucket list in our minds of what makes us lovable, successful, and worthy?

Now there's a second image. Take a deep breath with me as we reset the stage for this one.

The second picture God gave me is of a bike with training wheels. Do you remember those little training wheels you added to your bike as a kid so you wouldn't topple over? I can still remember cruising down the cul-de-sac in my little bike with pom poms on the handlebars, a big banana seat, and massive helmet that swallowed my face, feeling on top of the world as I wheeled past our neighbors' houses.

At first I thought training wheels sounded a little silly and rudimentary compared to a big Olympic-sized racing bike! Isn't that so simple, so *basic*?

But then the picture panned out. Imagine you're riding a bike with training wheels, but instead of riding uphill on this bumpy terrain, you're cruising slowly down a smoothly paved street on the other side of the mountain. This road has been there the whole time, but because you were so fixated on just getting up the hill and not falling off the bike, you didn't even notice there was a paved road at all.

As you look to your right, you see an expanse of ocean beyond you. It's an expansive beach right of a National Geographic catalog with bright turquoises, deep blues, and soft white foam. It's exquisite and heavenly.

Instead of dirt and grime, a salty ocean breeze blows through your hair. You feel refreshed, alive, and a deep peace floods your soul.

This is a picture of how it feels to partner with the Holy Spirit versus doing it in our own strength. This ride is downhill, not uphill. It's restful and full of delight and awe. The wheels represent extra support and stability so you know you won't fall.

The Psalms say it perfectly: "The Lord makes firm the steps of the one who delights in him; though he may stumble, he will not fall, for the Lord upholds him with his hand" (Psalm 37:23-24).

This ride is not exhausting, it's not a race, and in fact you hardly have to move your feet at all. You simply focus on gently steering the wheel down the path. No exertion, just rest, and a childlike awe.

When we rest in his Spirit, God fills us up instead of emptying us like the hustle does. We are clothed with dignity and strength and laugh without fear of the future rather than panting in exhaustion (Proverbs 31:25). This is how it can when we pursue God's call on our lives.

Yes, it's a journey. Yes, it's an adventure. And yes, we do have to pedal a little by moving forward step by step, but how much would you rather enjoy a restful journey than wrestle with yourself by constantly seeking to measure up to everyone else?

This is so important to realize now as you start your journey because there will always be countless ways to measure ourselves, our abilities, and our belongings to the people around us. Yet, Jesus only cares about our one and singular race that we complete with his help.

Friend, what I am learning (and I am still in it with you, I promise) is that most of us are on this uphill ride until we meet God and welcome the Holy Spirit. It's simply not sustainable without him.

Whether you want to start a nonprofit, run a business, raise a family, fill in the blank, if you do the thing in your own strength, it will surely exhaust you. You will hit more walls than you were intended to. You will burn out because you are carrying things that you weren't meant to carry in the first place. You're racing uphill after people who aren't even running your same race, and for what? Most of all, you will be depriving yourself the opportunity to *enjoy* and delight in the beauty of the journey God has invited you into.

Here are a few Scriptures that show us how the Holy Spirit can help us as we run (or bike or jog or walk) our God-destined race. These encourage me so much because they remind me that I don't have to hustle, and I certainly don't have to do it on my own.

In the Holy Spirit we have a helper and an intercessor.

> "In the same way, the Spirit helps us in our weakness. We do not know what we ought to pray for, but the Spirit himself intercedes for us through wordless groans. And he who searches our hearts knows the mind of the Spirit, because the Spirit intercedes for God's people in accordance with the will of God." (Romans 8:26-27)

In the Holy Spirit is all the strength, wisdom, and courage that we need. The Holy Spirit is a helper who teaches us, leads us, and reminds us of God's will for our lives.

> "But the Advocate, the Holy Spirit, whom the Father will send in my name, will teach you all things and will remind you of everything I have said to you." (John 14:26)

The Holy Spirit empowers us and leads us to do what is in God's will.

> "But you will receive power when the Holy Spirit comes on you; and you will be my witnesses in Jerusalem, and in all Judea and Samaria, and to the ends of the earth." (Acts 1:8)

The Holy Spirit enables us to bear good fruit and operate in spiritual gifts that help us to function as stronger and healthier leaders.

> "But the fruit of the Spirit is love, joy, peace, forbearance, kindness, goodness, faithfulness, gentleness and self-control... Since we live by the Spirit, let us keep in step with the Spirit." (Galatians 5:22- 25)

In my story, God let me take the uphill route until I burnt out. Let my journey be a cautionary tale: I took the impressive job, got the right degrees, travelled to countries and continents around the world, and ended up burning out with stress and a chronic auto-immune disorder. That was where my own strength brought me to my own end until I found a deeper healing in Christ. Let me save you some sweat; opting in is way easier.

CHAPTER 14

Cheer Squad

The next practice we're going to talk about is how to cultivate genuine community that can hold our dream with us and cheer us on in the journey. I'll never forget attending a writing retreat with the writing legend himself Bob Goff when he told us about a viral video of a flash mob. In the video, a woman was running through a park when a crowd of people holding signs came up behind her to cheer her on. The further she ran, the more people popped up out of nowhere to cheer for her by name and run alongside her. She might have started her run alone, but by the end of her route that day dozens of people were running alongside her. When we're pursuing a dream with God, isn't that kind of encouragement we all wish we had?

Being a Dream Carrier

We all have a God-sized dream, or maybe multiple dreams in our heart, but nobody ever prepared me for the cost of what the journey would entail. When we think about dreams, we often think about mountaintop moments, like speaking onstage in front of huge audiences, or gaining thousands of followers and building an online "platform" that finally earns you that blue checkmark. Maybe for you that's publishing your first book, having thriving relationships, building a family.

But the journey to get there before those dreams come to pass? Often it's a lonely journey, and it's gritty sometimes. The journey to becoming a leader can even be one of the loneliest we will ever face. In reality, it's because the distance between the *dream* and the *execution* can be the farthest distance you will ever run.

You might have so many people on your team, or others praying over you, cheering you on, and sowing into what you are doing. But you might also find yourself in a place like I was when I started The Well Initiative, just trying to boot strap and figure it out by myself.

When I first got married my husband went on a campaign to get me into sports. Growing up, I was not very athletic, and I was definitely not someone to religiously follow professional sports like football or basketball. Somewhere along the road, he realized the best way to get me into the game was to share stories of the players, like about their wives and their families, and that I loved some teams just because I like the colors in their uniforms! Oops!

He started telling me stories of the players and how they had to overcome their circumstances to get where they were. And that's when I really listened. Today I could write entire chapters about the athletes who persevered—not just physically, but also mentally—to see their dreams realized.

My husband's favorite player, Steph Curry, plays in the NBA for the Golden State Warriors. In addition to being called the greatest shooter in NBA history, he's considered one of the greatest basketball players of all time (unless maybe if you're a Lebron fan). Today he's a nine-time All-Star, has been named the NBA's Most Valuable Player (MVP) twice, and has won four NBA championships. The guy is like an automatic cannon! Literally every time he shoots from behind the three-point line, it seems like the ball always goes in. You want Steph on your team and you definitely don't want to be playing against him. But what I love about his story is that he didn't have success at first, just a dream.

When Steph first tried out for the NBA, college scouts assessed him as having "little to no ability" and that he would never excel at the NBA level. Can you imagine what it took to keep going, or how many thousands, or tens of thousands, of practice shots he had to shoot to get to where he is today?

Steph had a dream, and he didn't give up on it no matter what people said about him. He was what I call a *dream-carrier*. You may not be a big basketball fan, but it's no understatement to say he's gained his respect and proved those scouts wrong. Years later when Steph had found NBA fame, he shared in an interview something his mom told him when he was thirteen that carried him through. She told him: "Nobody writes the story except for you... So think real hard about it."

He added, "Anytime I've needed it—anytime I've been snubbed, or underrated, or even flat-out disrespected—I've just remembered those words, and I've persevered."

Through it all—the hate, the negativity, the countless people who doubted him—he *persevered*. Anyone who knows me knows I am way too short to play basketball! But what would it look like for us to keep reminding ourselves that we can't let others tell the story or tell us if our dreams are legitimate or not?

Jesus is our true story writer. And how much more can we trust his identity for us, his name for us, and his call for us, far and above what other people say about our dreams and purpose? If we are going to succeed, we are going to need to learn how to edit the voices we hear around us and find people who can run with us as we go after our dreams together.

Who Is Your Elizabeth?

At the beginning, the world around you isn't going to see the very thing you are carrying. The people around you—including the closest ones—might see glimpses of your dream, but it will only be a glimpse. Only God and you, the dream-carrier, will be able to see the full picture of what's going on inside.

The journey of *dream carrying* is a key part of our leadership journey. Leaders are meant to be visionaries who can carry something—or maybe some people—forward, but that means there is always a gap. Hold onto that dream and let it be stewarded well so that it can grow before others see it?

There is nothing natural about carrying a God-dream because it's bigger than our own.

It is a supernatural vision. It will be carried out in a supernatural way. This journey doesn't have to be a lonely one if we can find other dream-carriers to journey with.

When Mary became pregnant, I can't imagine how overwhelmed she must have felt. She must have considered things like: Will Joseph leave me? Will my family disown me? How will I get through pregnancy, never mind raising a child? Will we have the finances to care for a baby? Will I be a good mom? Can I do it? Why did God trust me? Did he mean this for someone else?

But we're told that God sent her to be with another dream-carrier.

> As the angel delivered the news to Mary that she was to carry baby Jesus who would be the Son of the Most High, she asks: "How will this be, since I am a virgin?" (Luke 1:34)

Here's what the rest of the passage says.

> The angel then answered, "The Holy Spirit will come on you, and the power of the Most High will overshadow you. So the holy one to be born will be called[b] the Son of God. Even Elizabeth your relative is going to have a child in her old age, and she who was said to be unable to conceive is

in her sixth month. For no word from God will ever fail."

"I am the Lord's servant," Mary answered. "May your word to me be fulfilled." Then the angel left her. (Luke 1:35-38)

The Lord knew in his graciousness that she would need someone to carry the dream—and literally, a baby—alongside her. How redemptively miraculous was it that Elizabeth too, who in her old age also shouldn't have been able to conceive?

And now for the best part of the story!

At that time Mary got ready and hurried to a town in the hill country of Judea, where she entered Zechariah's home and greeted Elizabeth. When Elizabeth heard Mary's greeting, the baby leaped in her womb, and Elizabeth was filled with the Holy Spirit. In a loud voice she exclaimed: "Blessed are you among women, and blessed is the child you will bear! But why am I so favored, that the mother of my Lord should come to me? As soon as the sound of your greeting reached my ears, the baby in my womb leaped for joy. Blessed is she who has believed that the Lord would fulfill his promises to her!" (Luke 1:39-45)

I just love how the Scripture highlights how Elizabeth's baby leapt for joy in her womb when it heard Mary's greeting.

Have you ever had that feeling of sharing a dream with someone who truly *gets it?* It's a deep feeling of joy—feeling understood and seen at the same time in a way that so few others can. It's also a relief sometimes that they

Finding our fellow dream-carriers is an essential part of the process.

share the same passion or see the same need as you. It's the feeling of "I'm not crazy! They see it too!" Finding our fellow dream-carriers is an essential part of the process.

So, as you begin your journey, I encourage you to ask yourself: who is your Elizabeth? The enemy's biggest and best tool is to keep us hidden and alone. Imagine how much Mary might have struggled without someone who understood her dream-carrying in that season of pregnancy. Being with Elizabeth wasn't just a simple encouragement or arrangement, it was a God-given, divinely appointed way to come alongside her.

When Relationships Change

As important as it is to find others who will dream with us, I also want to get real about finding friendships and a community who will walk through the messy journey of leadership with us until our dreams finally come to pass. These friendships can be really tricky, and sometimes we get hurt along the way. Sometimes this is another "wall" we might face.

I have learned that just like seasons, our friendships will change. The very friends who carry us through one specific season—like high school, or college, or living in a specific city—may or may not be assigned to be part of our inner circle of friendships as we grow. Looking back, I think that even *anticipating* that natural change, in friendships just as in life, would have saved me from so much pain. Here are a few ways I've seen relationships transform and some tips to find your own tribe.

The "Used To" Friend

The first challenge we faced was that there were many friends who didn't understand what we had been called to and thought we should change directions. Many of them still saw us as the way we were when we were walking through a specific season with them, and understandably so. They saw us exactly in the ways they were "used to"—as in we "used to" do things together, we "used to" share certain friendships in common, you get the idea.

Have you ever had friendships like this, that seem frozen in one point in time? Some of these well-meaning friends thought we were giving up so many of the great things we had in our former life and in some ways, they were right. When we lived in LA, where we met, we had such a rich community. On paper we had all the foundations we needed to be successful. It made perfect sense we'd stay in that setting until God asked us to change directions.

I can almost guarantee you that there will be people who don't understand and even think you're doing something that is unwise, wrong, or even irresponsible. God's ways never look the way the world does, so there's a natural fault line between both realities. But there are also times Jesus will ask us to walk away from what's comfortable, even *logical,* to build your next chapter, and that's what happened to us. Even though we had spent so much time building our lives in one place, God had an entirely new reality in mind for us.

Luke 14 paints a picture for us of what it looks like to turn away from our "used to" reality. Luke 14:25 says, "Large crowds were traveling with Jesus, and turning to them he said: 'If anyone comes to me and does not hate father and mother, wife and children, brothers and sisters—yes, even their own life—such a person cannot be my disciple. And whoever does not carry their cross and follow me cannot be my disciple.'"

The first time I read this passage I thought it was so harsh. How could a good God call us to hate a parent, sibling, spouse, or our beloved children? Aren't those all good gifts from the Lord? And how could he ask us to even hate our own precious life when he created and knew us, before we were even in the womb? How could he possibly say those things if he's a God of love?

Now that I look at it though, I think it's really a verse about seasons where the Lord redirects us.

If I could put it into my own words what I think he's really saying here is: "My children, I want you to look hard at your life right now. You see those things that are most precious to you, like your father and mother you depend on and your wife or child whom you love? I want to be so central and so elevated in your life that you love me even more. I want to be the closest, most important person in your life far and above any other relationship that you have."

I imagine him saying this with so much passion, compassion, and longing to be with us in his eyes. In my imagination he pauses to study our face as he says, "I want to be your everything. When my disciples come and follow me, it is a whole of life negotiation. Nothing else left out. I want every piece of your life, and that is what it looks like to truly carry your cross and follow me. It's all in, all chips on the table, and I want to come in and do the rest."

With these relationships, our friends aren't calling us to necessarily do something bad, but they simply don't understand the new direction Jesus is taking us. It's hard to see it even ourselves why God is redirecting us sometimes when we haven't yet seen the fruit of it. Yet if we are true disciples of Jesus, we will have to be all in and leave the familiar time and time again. We are invited into a constant and consistent surrender of ourselves and even the things most precious to us to find the thing most precious in all of the world—Jesus himself.

Mission Creep

On the journey of building a God-sized dream as a leader there's almost always another type of relationship that comes up. I call that the "opinionated friend." Anytime we're starting something new or visionary, there are always going to be people who will want to speak into it. That's well and good, but the problem is that when we elevate other people's voices and opinions over God, we lose sight of the purpose we've been called to.

In the military, they call this kind of drifting "mission creep." The Oxford Dictionary defines mission creep as "a gradual shift in objectives during the course of a military campaign, often resulting in an unplanned long-term commitment." In other words, you might feel strongly like God is asking you to act in a certain direction, but over time as we start inviting other people's opinions, we drift away from our initial vision.

I love this term because this is exactly what happens when we have so many voices around us telling us which way to go. And if we listen long enough, we will actually end up far off course pursuing other commitments we were never supposed to pursue to begin with.

When I was first started The Well Initiative, this was something that majorly blindsided me. As someone who's naturally a bit of a people pleaser, I was so excited to share my new vision with people only to see that many of them had opinions and critiques. Occasionally a few people even seemed to suggest that my work would be obsolete. I went from being so passionate and determined to feeling defeated, lost, and confused. I was utterly crushed. *Surely*, I thought, *if these other people I'm sharing with are believers, they'll also catch the vision and want to come alongside what I'm doing, right?*

What I've found is that if we're not totally in step with the Father at every point, we will experience mission creep. While again, so many of these people were well-meaning, I had to learn that as a leader, and especially as a founder, I would need to guard my vision and ask the Holy Spirit for discernment of who to share with at every part of the journey.

Some days, it was just me and Jesus, or me and my husband sitting in pajamas on the couch. Then slowly but surely I started to find my people. The best relationships in the pioneering phase were friendships with people who would pray over me, offer encouragement, and help me seek the Father's voice as the blueprint unfolded.

Can you think of people like that in your life right now, or do you need to pray for new relationships that will keep you focused on Jesus as you build? If you're not sure, I suggest sharing a small piece of what you're doing with a few friends and see how they respond. As you build trust in sharing this new endeavor, start to share more. Your people are the ones whose eyes light up as you share, who might ask thoughtful and at times challenging questions, but who wholeheartedly connect with the passion and fire you feel in your core most often because it connects with their own story.

One last thing, not everyone is meant to be on this part of the journey with you. Some friends might be amazing cheerleaders further down the road. Maybe they might even be part of your team one day, and they have incredible talent that will bless your organization in years to come.

But at the very beginning, keep your circle tight just like Jesus did. Yes, he had twelve disciples and many crowds followed him as he spoke. But he also had an inner group—composed of Simon Peter, John, and James—that he relied on throughout his ministry and who were ultimately there with him in the garden of Gethsemane right before his death.

These three were among the first disciples and followed him the longest. They saw Jesus raise Jairus' daughter from the dead, walked with him through his darkest times, and were the only disciples to witness Jesus' transfiguration (Mark 9:2-3). They were flawed, but for some reason Jesus singled them out of the group to be his closest confidants along the way.

Protect your vision and let God bring the right people to walk with you from the very beginning.

Running From Sauls

Every time we receive a powerful call from the Lord, we know there will be an enemy working to oppose the ways of the kingdom. That shouldn't surprise us, but what I didn't expect along the journey is that the enemy might use other people—even other Christians—to varying degrees to try to shut down your vision. This is what happened to David. David was discovered when he was young and told he would be the next king, but King Saul grew jealous of him. First Samuel 18:7 says, "As they danced, they sang: 'Saul has slain his thousands, and David his tens of thousands.'" Saul became so envious of David's strength that he ultimately tried to kill him. Now that is some serious opposition!

Now, this is an extreme example, but we need to be aware that opposition can come, and it may even come from the places we least expect it. On the outside, Saul represented every kind of worldly success. He was described as a man of wealth who was tall and good-looking, "as handsome a young man as could be found anywhere in Israel" (1 Samuel 9:2). He was a powerful leader who had led his nation through a series of military conquests. And yet, we see his heart was deeply sick and he did not honor God.

In my journey it looked like prominent Christian leaders who wanted me to build their ministries but wouldn't support my call because it would take away from what they were doing. It has looked like others slandering my work and speaking against me because I didn't fold under pressure. It was deeply painful and at many times made me want to give up on ministry and the church altogether.

When these things happen, we must keep our hearts soft and be quick to forgive. Unforgiveness and bitterness become a poison in our hearts when they are not dealt with. I've seen the fruit of it in leaders' lives who have not forgiven and have bled out onto those they were called to shepherd. I've even heard a prominent mentor share that unforgiveness is the number one thing that will destroy our ministries far quicker than any public "moral failure" might.

Hence this is one of the greatest challenges of the Christian life—forgive freely and pray regularly for your friends and your enemies to be blessed. I firmly believe that if we deal with this unforgiveness and bitterness quickly and with seriousness, your ministry and work will be blessed for it. God will bring justice in his own ways. Our job is to forgive.

> Jesus told us that "in this world you will have trouble" (John 16:33), so it's not shocking that this can come through man. And yet we are also reminded in James 1:2-3: "Consider it pure joy, my brothers and sisters, whenever you face trials of many kinds, because you know that the testing of your faith produces perseverance."

As you think about your own journey, who are the people who are going to truly cheer you on as you run your race? Relationships will change, not everyone will believe in you, and you might even have a few spears thrown your way. But if you find the right people, then you will run a lot further than you ever could on your own.

CHAPTER 15

Humble Pie

Hundreds of men lift their hands in the air singing, as Maverick City Music's "I Thank God" echoes through the room.

They sing in a loud, united baritone. Banners bearing the fruits of the Spirit—love, joy, peace, patience—hang boldly against the stark concrete walls, a visual reminder that transformation is possible. The room buzzes with passion as the drums quicken and the energy surges.

You can feel it in the air—a rush of joy and holy surrender. These men aren't just singing the lyrics; they're pouring out the deepest cries of their hearts. Others dance and praise. There is a palpable sense of celebration in the air.

It's the most incredible, life-changing worship service I've ever attended. But it's not in a megachurch with a considerable production team—there are no LED lights, fog machines, giant audio speakers, or celebrity pastors. Instead, I hear a simple acoustic guitar as I watch a sanctuary full of men all wearing blue, crying out to the Lord.

This is what revival looks like inside a maximum-security prison once named one of the most dangerous prisons in America. And yet, the Holy Spirit is in the room in a way I've never experienced before. It's what I believe every church's atmosphere should feel like.

To be servants, to be humbled, we have to be broken down.

One of the craziest examples I've ever seen of someone being broken down and turned into a leader is a man by the name of Luther Collie. My husband, Chad, is a filmmaker and over the course of the last few years, I've had the privilege of coming alongside him as he wrote, directed, and produced a film about a man who found Christ behind bars.

Luther was sentenced to twenty-five years in prison as a young man after committing an armed robbery to fund a music studio. Talk about hitting a wall and bring broken down.

Luther was at the lowest point of his life and felt like his life was over.

He had been an up-and-coming rap artist in Miami, and after many closed doors, he felt desperate and did something that changed the trajectory of his life—but not in the way you might think. Days after he got behind bars, he had a radical encounter with Christ when he ran into an old childhood friend who offered to pray for him at the prison.

He spent the next two decades at one of the worst prisons in the state of Florida as a pastor, bringing encouragement, hope, and healing to men at their lowest point and in their darkest hour. He even went on to get married, start a family, get a master's degree in theology, and teach business classes—all while imprisoned until he was finally released in early 2025. His life, if you really look at it, is fuller than so many people who aren't in jail.

Because of his faithfulness, supernatural miracles happened as marriages were healed, addictions were broken, families grown, and so many men set free. The prison experienced such a large revival that Maverick City even recorded an album there and countless Christian leaders have visited to see what God is doing.

Luther's story is one of radical faith and humility. To be in the darkest place–yet still hold tightly onto the hope of the gospel. What is so interesting about attending church in Luther's former prison, too, is that people wear their scars and not their badges of pride on Sunday. There's no airs about getting dressed up or what people are wearing, no judgement, no flashing lights. Just an acoustic guitar and the acapella voices of a room of men or women who have truly tasted what grace is. Although they still have to face the consequences of their actions, the grace of God has still met them in their lowest point. Through Luther I have learned freedom is actually a mindset and condition of the heart rather than a condition of our circumstances. Like the Apostle Paul, who was imprisoned for his faith, Luther learned to be joyful in *all* circumstances and that humility and surrender are the way to the cross.

The Bible tells us that true humility is found in the awe and fear of the Lord. Scripture tells us in Romans 12:3, "Do not think of yourself more highly than you ought, but rather think of yourself with sober judgment, in accordance with the faith God has distributed to each of you." We can think all day about what we want to do or create, but when God enters the picture, our agendas will change. Sometimes when we're hitting a wall it's because God wants to teach us humility.

As leaders we must get to the place where we will say, "God, I'll go anywhere you want me to go!" Where must authentically declare, "Less of me, and more of you, Jesus! Who and where can I serve?" True servant leadership is always about God's agenda over our own.

Lastly, humility uproots what's underneath the surface. Chances are, if you struggle with humility, you might have some pride in one area of your life. We all do. Yet as someone once shared with me, sin makes sense. You see, psychologists tell us that if we have pride, we are afraid. Pride happens where we are afraid to be seen as inadequate in a certain area of our life. To work around that fear, we will prop up the places and try to control the areas where we have learned to find love, acceptance, value, and safety.

For example, say you're someone who struggles with perfectionism (same here). You might control certain areas of your life, from grades to your appearance, to reach that standard you've set for yourself.

But God wants to free us from that fear and pride so we can grow in humility as leaders. To our fears, he asks us to trust him.

Submitting to him and being humbled? It's not a punishment. It's the beginning of our freedom in Christ, and it's a front row seat to see him move where we are weakest.

Facing a wall—being humbled—is never easy, but if we can endure there's a "great cloud of witnesses" that will be cheering you on as we are grown into Kingdom leaders along the way.

PART V

SET FREE TO LEAD

CHAPTER 16

The Break Before the Breakthrough

It was spring 2024. Chad and I looked at each other across the couch and realized we needed to pray.

We had been feeling unsettled in Dallas for some time and believed God was about to do something new in our lives. It felt oddly familiar to times I was called to India, first moved to DC, and, more recently, like when we moved to Dallas. The ground was shaking once again.

We had the idea to pray in separate rooms, then compare notes, and see what the new thing might be. You can imagine my surprise when I *thought* God would say we should join a new small group. He actually told us that it was time to move back to LA, where we had first met. Even more shocking, we felt strongly that he asked us to move there within three months.

Sometimes we don't always understand why God is asking us to do something, but it's a crucial part of our story coming together. We did move in three months—and little did I know that it would be a major moment before a breakthrough would come. But more on that later...

Learning from Joshua

One of my favorite books in the Bible that teaches us about the leadership journey is the book of Joshua. Joshua is the sixth book in the Old Testament. It tells the story of how the Israelites took possession of the land of Canaan and the division of the land across the twelve tribes of Israel. I love it because it shows us the inner workings behind God's faithfulness, and it introduces us to Joshua, a faithful leader who also hit some "walls" in his journey but persisted until a breakthrough happened.

Joshua was the successor to Moses, who had just led the Israelites out of Egypt. As you read the book of Joshua, the first six chapters outline how he steps in as a leader after Moses and leads his army in a series of epic battles, including one of the most famous battles we see in the Old Testament where God instructs them to take Jericho.

By this point they've taken out multiple kings and seen the faithfulness of God, and yet Jericho is the most significant plot of land because it represents the promises God has spoken to the Israelites and their future home.

God tells Joshua to have the men walk around the city once a day for seven days, and finally on the seventh day they're instructed to scream and shout until the walls come down. It's an epic story. If you haven't read it before, you need to!

And yet what's so interesting to me is that after his *biggest* victory as a leader, the moment he and his troops have been waiting for, Joshua hits a wall and he's ready to give up completely.

The Break

Scripture tells us: "Then Joshua tore his clothes and fell facedown to the ground before the ark of the Lord, remaining there till evening. The elders of Israel did the same, and sprinkled dust on their heads" (Joshua 7:6).

This guy is at his absolute wit's end. Have you ever felt like this, like just giving up completely and putting your face in the dirt (or maybe the carpet in your room)? I definitely have. I did when God told us we had to uproot our whole lives again in just a few months! Some days I'm like Joshua in chapter 6, feeling strong, courageous, and emboldened, like I'm ready to go into battle.

And some days it feels like life is pure chaos. The Bible says he was so distraught he stayed there for the entire day and even tore his clothes in agony. Wow. Joshua was really not having it, and his team was feeling it too! Now don't miss this next part. He starts talking to God about it.

Joshua says:

> Alas, Sovereign Lord, why did you ever bring this people across the Jordan to deliver us into the hands of the Amorites to destroy us? If only we had been content to stay on the other side of the Jordan! Pardon your servant, Lord. What can I say, now that Israel has been routed by its enemies? The Canaanites and the other people of the country will hear about this and they will surround us and wipe out our name from the earth. What then will you do for your own great name? (Joshua 7:7)

Joshua's crying out to God. Here's really asking, "What's going on? Why has this been so hard, God? I thought you said you had us, why didn't you have our back?"

And then: "We should have stayed where we were."

Here's the Amy Standard Translation: "God, why is this happening to me? Can we even trust you? Here we were, trying to be obedient and faithful, and look where it's landed us! What the heck are you doing here?!"

Oh yeah. I've been there, done that. Have you stepped out in obedience, only to have things come crashing down around you? Hit a million roadblocks? Doubted God's character, his faithfulness, and goodness? Felt like he wasn't on your side, or even that he lied to you or forgot about you? 10,000%. I can still remember bringing home boxes from Home Depot, looking across our living room to see a sea of belongings that needed to be packed, and thinking, "God, this is a bad idea." Don't even get me started on the number of times I asked God what the Dallas season was about in the first place.

After this moment of despair, God steps in. He lets Joshua feel his feelings, including letting him feel his anger towards God. Then, we read:

> The Lord said to Joshua, "Stand up! What are you doing down on your face? Israel has sinned; they have violated my covenant, which I commanded them to keep. They have taken some of the devoted things; they have stolen, they have lied, they have put them with their own possessions. That is why the Israelites cannot stand against their enemies; they turn their backs and run because they have been made liable to destruction. I will not be with you anymore unless you destroy whatever among you is devoted to destruction."
> (Joshua 7:10-12)

God sees Joshua in his mess and says to him, "Stand up! What are you doing on your face?" I feel like this is even more significant. In the bigger picture, I just imagine he also wants to say: "Keep going! You can do this! You have me by your side!"

It's after that that God steps in and fulfills his promises to the Israelites fully.

The Breakthrough

Because of Joshua's faithfulness to stand up and keep going, the Israelites eventually claim the land of Canaan and they finally settle in the Promised Land. At the end of his life, Joshua declares, "Every promise has been fulfilled; not one has failed" (Joshua 23: 14). Then, as he assembles all of Israel for his last words, he recounts how God has moved:

> I am very old. You yourselves have seen everything the Lord your God has done to all these nations for your sake; it was the Lord your God who fought for you. Remember how I have allotted as an inheritance for your tribes all the land of the nations that remain—the nations I conquered—between the Jordan and the Mediterranean Sea in the west. The Lord your God himself will push them out for your sake. He will drive them out before you, and you will take possession of their land, as the Lord your God promised you. Be very strong; be careful to obey all that is written in the Book of the Law of Moses, without turning aside to the right or to the left. Do not associate with these nations that remain among you; do not invoke the names of their gods or swear by them. You must not serve them or bow down to them. But you are to hold fast to the Lord your God, as you have until now. (Joshua 23:2-8)

After years in exile from Egypt, through Moses' leadership, and now Joshua's, the Lord was faithful. Indeed, we see that:

- God's promises to Israel over many years were fulfilled.

- Tens of thousands experienced God's provision, and God's people were given a new home.

- Enemies were stopped in their tracks.

- Generational curses were broken.

- Legacy was established.

The moment when Joshua stood up was more than just physically pulling himself off the ground. It was a prophetic announcement declaring that he was going to keep going. In it, Joshua showed his team and the rest of the Israelites that as a leader he was going to believe God was who he said he was, that his promises to Israel were true, and that they were going to keep going.

The Challenge to Stand

This passage has meant so much to me in my own leadership journey at times I've wanted to give up and throw in the towel completely. If that's you, you're in good company along with Joshua, who himself was even described as one of the most courageous and successful leaders over Israel.

Is it possible that there is a bit of Joshua in you? So many leaders in the body of Christ are feeling discouraged, frustrated, and tired as they seek the promises of God over their lives. They're having their own Joshua moment ten times over. I've felt it too.

Others are feeling like everyone else around them is experiencing a breakthrough, and their breakthrough will never come. We are asking, "Where is the promise you gave me, God? Where is my spouse, my child, my career breakthrough? Will you do it for me, too, God?"

We're about to throw in the towel and feel tempted to settle because the hope we once held so closely has been waning in this long waiting season, leaving us tired and weary.

Yet through it all, I believe God is more than able to take our heavy feelings. And even in spite of them, he's about to move in a massive way to uproot old systems of religion and bring a fresh outpouring of his spirit in our lives and in the global church around the world.

What do you think God's invitation for you might be in the waiting? Here's my best guess.

What has felt like a season of delay or God forgetting about us is actually him doing a deeper work that will bring sanctification, and a stirring up of tired systems that must be refreshed for his Spirit to fall and bring freedom, redemption, and a deeper heart change.

I'm praying that he is going to restore your hope. I believe his encouragement to us today is, "My child! Keep going! The pressure is always going to be most intense before your breakthrough moment."

What could come from your decision to stand up and keep going today? Like Joshua, I bet you are so close to your breakthrough.

Exercise

When we decide to stand up and run our race, we announce in the heavenly realms that we're running on the offensive for the kingdom of God. If you're feeling stuck or simply overwhelmed today, here's what I work through on my bad days (hey, we all have them).

1.) Be still and silent with God for five minutes. Put your phone and screens in another room, and start by just listening with no agenda, asking him to quiet any other voices. If you're struggling to be still, try listening to worship music and let the lyrics wash over you.

Let yourself rest in Jesus' loving presence and allow the words to soak in.

2.) Thank God for his faithfulness in your life. Reflect and make a list of what he's done for you, and how he's answered your prayers in the past. This is so essential because the enemy's biggest plot against us is to make us question God's character, so we must always remember how he's been faithful.

3.) Pray. Be real with God about your feelings and cry out to him. Ask for faith, strength, and boldness against the enemy or any opposition you might be facing.

4.) Allow God to respond to you. Ask him how he feels about you and your circumstances, and what he's doing. Write this response down if you can.

5.) Declare Scripture over your circumstances. It's important to speak this *out loud* to yourself! The Bible tells us in Ephesians 6 to put on the full armor of God, and his Word is our greatest weapon.

6.) Meditate on God's promises over your life. Write them out, declare them, put them on Post-Its around the house. Here are some to get you started:

- God is faithful in all He does (Psalm 33:4).

- He will never leave or forsake you (Deuteronomy 3:18).

- God works all things together for the good of those who love him (Romans 8:28).

- He has adopted you into his kingdom and given you a spiritual inheritance (Ephesians 1:5).

- Goodness and mercy will follow you all the days of your life (Psalm 23:6).

- There is nothing we can do to separate ourselves from God's love (Romans 8:38).

Keep going. Decide you're not going to leave the Lord's presence until you've heard from him and feel his peace and presence over you and any lies you might be believing.

Don't give up on the promises God has spoken over you. You're so close.

CHAPTER 17

The Twelve-Year Journey

Remember that dream God gave me back in India to start a nonprofit called The Well Initiative?

I would later learn that it wouldn't happen for three months or even three years. In fact, I formally launched our first program in 2025–*twelve years later*–and as everything in my life was literally burning down to the ground.

It happened like this: the essentials were in place. I had started to put everything into process in 2022 when we lived in Dallas, like setting up a 501(c)3, defining our vision, building a website, creating our initial branding and marketing materials, and so on. I had even met with several leaders in the field to share about our work.

After *years* of carrying the dream with God, I sensed him telling me it was time to launch our first program overseas. Our flagship leadership program, The Well Initiative Academy, was about to be launched in Uganda in partnership with a nonprofit called Bringing Hope to the Family.

Through this program, we planned to train over one hundred students, most of them former orphans, in a unique, year-long leadership development program. Just like my vision of the Samaritan woman at the well, my dream was that this program would not only communicate to these women their value and identity in Christ, but they would learn real, practical, leadership skills like public speaking, writing, and how to tell their own stories of healing and resilience. At the end of the program, each student would create an action plan to serve their communities with their God-given purpose, and the winning proposals would be awarded microgrants so that students could start their own small businesses. The goal was to expand it to other countries with the hope of empowering female trafficking survivors.

I could never have imagined what would happen next. The day we finally opened up our fundraising page to raise funds for this new program—I'm not kidding—the *very* second I clicked the "Launch" button, we received a call from our doctor. He shared that my husband and I had contracted RSV. We needed to quarantine away from our families for Christmas.

Then, two weeks later was January 7, 2025. National news. One of the worst wildfires in California's history. My entire hometown burned to the ground.

The Well Initiative, and our first international program, was finally birthed out of the fire.

Teacups are made in a kiln so they can withstand high temperatures. My dream was too.

Three Months Later

How do you begin to move forward from a great loss like the fires our family faced? How, when just the day before you were living your life like just another day, could your entire world be gone in twenty-four hours?

As I write this conclusion, it's been three months since the fires to the day. The irony isn't lost on me that I was looking for words to talk about leadership in adversity when we faced it in such a big way myself. In fact, it all happened days before my original book deadline (a big thank you to my incredible editor Mikaela for being so kind to push back my deadline until we sorted things out).

I don't have all the answers, and we are still taking things day by day even as I write this, but here is what I have learned about leadership so far and what it looks like to carry a dream through the fire.

Lessons in the Fire

Believe it or not, I have learned that losing everything does not actually break you. When the worst-case scenario happens, it's not actually the *end*. It's a lesson that I never thought I would have to learn, but it wasn't until we really lost everything that I realized what is most valuable in life.

I can truly and honestly say that even when the worst thing imaginable happens and you lose everything, if you have Jesus you have everything you need. This isn't a cheesy slogan, but rather a lesson learned with a lot of blood, sweat, and tears from grief.

Instead, I've learned firsthand from my family and the thousands of neighbors around us in LA that lost homes that week that it's not actually losing everything that breaks us, but the small things that add up over time. We can physically lose everything, but if we have a strong community and love around us, it's possible to rebuild. It's actually possible to keep going, and you know what? Even if it's not the road we imagined we'd walk down, we can come out stronger than when we started.

I think it's really the *smaller* things that will really bring us down. It's the things that deplete our *souls,* that kill and deafen our spirits, that are the most volatile. It's the way we push God aside and try to make it on our own, running from him instead of *to* him when our pain feels like too much to bear. It's in the ways we endlessly pursue things like success, wealth, and power, that will truly drain our souls because they will never fully satisfy us like Jesus could.

It's also not lost on me that as the fires struck, God would call me to start a nonprofit called The Well Initiative that was all about the living water that Jesus first offered the Samaritan woman at the well. In a city—and in a world—where we are always crying out for more, to "make something of ourselves," what does it look like for us to be led by Jesus?

There is something freeing in knowing that if we could get through that, our community can get through anything. What we thought would break us made us stronger. It didn't. We grew. And the enemy lost.

So, dear reader, as you look out onto this crazy journey called life and reflect on your own story and the dreams in your own heart, I have an audacious question for you: How do we continue to build as we examine the ashes in our own lives?

I pray you will never experience what we did this year. And yet, if you are facing something that feels like the end of life as you know it right now, I have hope that you can get through it too. What I have learned and seen in all of it is that if we don't have trials and adversity, we will never learn anything or grow.

What if the ashes you are currently standing in the middle of are the very place that will birth the precious dream that you carry?

My prayer is that you find your own teacups in the ashes and that you will see your dream come to pass, regardless of the adversity you face. You were made for this moment.

"Now to him who is able to do immeasurably more than all we ask or imagine, according to his power that is at work within us."
(Ephesians 3:20)

As devastating as this tragedy was, it taught me that God is to be found even in the ashes of our darkest seasons. Pictured above are my beloved teacups from India that we found on the day we sorted through the ashes of our old home. While everything else was unrecognizable, we found these cups perched delicately over the ashes and in almost perfect condition.

A close-up of my cups found in the rubble. These are the tea cups we would drink from as we shared with others about Jesus. Other neighbors in our community found items in their ashes that similarly defied logic. One family nearby reported finding three children's Bibles with every page intact, even when their home was a total loss. In a Catholic Church called Corpus Christi, 14 delicate stained glass windows representing the Stations of the Cross and the Blessed Sacrament of the Tabernacle were found untouched. Additionally, one neighbor who stayed in their house to defend it stepped outside to see crosses drawn in ash all the way around their home. Some say it's all ashes; I say they are filled with miracles.

Acknowledgements

First and foremost, I want to thank Jesus. This book is the result of so many prayers and a deep belief that he equips those he calls. I am so thankful for his grace, love, faithfulness, and presence that changed my life.

To all the people the Lord placed in my life to help carry this story forward—thank you. Your encouragement, wisdom, and love have meant more than words can say.

This book wouldn't have been possible without the support of my husband and best friend, Chad. Chad—thank you for always being my biggest cheerleader. You believed in this project even before I did. You've spent so many hours patiently reading my manuscript, brainstorming ideas, and you always knew exactly when I needed a pep talk to keep going (an extra bonus for your amazing sports stories)! I love you from the bottom of my heart, and I love every day with you. I am so very thankful that God gave me you and I couldn't imagine a better partner.

To my editor, Mikaela—working with you has been such a blessing. Your insights, attention to detail, and thoughtful suggestions helped shape this manuscript into something far better than I could have done. You made this process so much more approachable (and way more fun!). I never could have imagined when we first met that this book on leadership in adversity would be shaped by the fires, and you have been so flexible and gracious as our family picked up the pieces. Thank you for your honesty, grace and genuine care for the heart of this book.

To my family—Thank you for supporting me during the writing process. Ever since I was a little girl you have always encouraged me to write. You provided a strong foundation for us girls so that we could go out into the world and follow our dreams, and for that I am so grateful. I love you!

To my friends—Thank you for celebrating the small wins with me and reminding me to laugh and live life beyond the page. A special thanks to Kaylah and our women's group for your help coming up with my title!

To our church family—Your prayers in this process have truly meant the world to me. Thank you for reminding me that I have a story to tell and for encouraging me to keep going. A special thanks to Becky Jones and our fellow WILD leaders, my incredible Propel Women cohort, and our School of Discipleship group. Through the ups and downs of life you've helped carry us and you've encouraged me to keep growing as a leader.

To Leo—You made me laugh on days when I was out of steam and you remind me to pause, breathe, and be present in the moment!

To everyone who offered a kind word, a fresh perspective, or a much-needed break along the way—thank you. I am deeply grateful.

And finally, to the reader holding this book in your hands—I am so incredibly honored that you would offer your time to reading this book. My hope and prayer is that these pages would speak life and encouragement into your heart, and that you would feel the love of Jesus. You are so deeply loved and you hold so much purpose that the world needs.

With all my love and gratitude,
Amy

About the Author

Amy Smathers is the founder and CEO of *The Well Initiative*, a nonprofit that supports vulnerable women globally through leadership development and economic empowerment. Over the course of more than a decade, she has worked at the intersection of leadership, global development, and social impact, including working in the U.S. State Department, U.S. Institute of Peace, Human Rights Watch, and the Global Philanthropy Group. Amy is deeply passionate about empowering women to live freely in their God-given calling and mobilizing the church to address the world's most pressing challenges, from human trafficking to global poverty. She and her husband live in Los Angeles, California.

Get In Touch with Amy:

Instagram: @amy.smathers

Website: amysmathers.com

Learn More About The Well Initiative:

Website: wellinitiative.org

www.ingramcontent.com/pod-product-compliance
Lightning Source LLC
Chambersburg PA
CBHW020159090426
42734CB00008B/874